This handbook is dedicated to all the brave and adventurous individuals stepping into their own kitchens for the first time.

May this guide be your companion as you discover the joy and satisfaction of creating meals that nourish
both body and soul.

Here's to delicious beginnings and the confidence to cook up your own culinary adventures.

Copyright © 2024 by M.J. Lacombe
All rights reserved. No part of this book may be reproduced in any manner whatsoever without written permission except in the case of brief quotations embodied in critical articles and reviews.
First Printing, 2024
ISBN: 979-8-218-45209-4

Prologue

In her third year of college, our 20-year-old daughter faced a new challenge: feeding herself without the familiar comforts of home-cooked meals, prepaid cafeteria plans, or sorority house dinners. She was embarking on a journey of culinary independence, and she needed guidance. The internet is a treasure trove of intricate recipes, but when it comes to finding simple, essential information for everyday nourishment, it can feel like searching for a needle in a haystack.

This book is the result of our daughter's countless questions, often sent in frantic texts from the aisles of her local supermarket. Within these pages, you'll find not only answers but also a healthy dose of unsolicited advice – the kind that comes from parents who care deeply. "Intro to Food" doesn't require any prior knowledge, and it covers the basics of food shopping, preparation, and cooking.

Treat this book as a guide, not a rigid syllabus (except the chapter about kitchen safety – memorize that section). Otherwise, if there's something you don't like, skip it. If you have allergies, avoid it altogether. And always remember to drink plenty of water, be kind to yourself, and don't fret too much. Life has a funny way of sorting itself out.

So, welcome to "Intro to Food". We don't intend to turn you into a gourmet chef overnight. Instead, we wish to equip you with the practical knowledge and confidence you need to navigate the world of cooking as an independent adult. We're a friendly guide, a helping hand, and a source of comfort for those moments when you find yourself standing in front of the stove, wondering where to begin. Let's embark on this delicious journey together!

Intro to Food

M.J. LACOMBE

Contents

Dedication		i
Prologue		iii
1	From Plate to Heart	1
2	Resourceful Cooking	5
3	Kitchen Kickstart	9
4	Invest in Quality	25
5	Stretching the Shelf	43
6	Safe Bites	59
7	The Art of Time	67
8	Heat Masters	77
9	Effortless Eats	85
10	Boiled Eggs	87
11	4-Ingredient Salads	93
12	Salad Dressing/Dip/Marinade	105
13	Simple Tuna Salad Recipe	111
14	Hearty Lentil Soup	115
15	Baked Potato	121
16	Bolognese Sauce	125
17	Baked Chicken Breast	131
18	Elevate Your Cooking Game	137

VIII ~ *PROLOGUE*

19	Beyond the Basics - Shrimp Dish	145
20	Beyond the Basics - Curry Dish	151
21	Resources	159
22	Notes	163

INTRO TO FOOD

Chapter 1
From Plate to Heart

How Food Fosters Connection

In the late 1970s, a man with an incredible appetite made headlines. Michel Lotito, better known as Monsieur Mangetout, amazed the world with his unique eating abilities. Unlike the strongmen of the circus, Lotito's talent lay in consuming things you wouldn't typically find on a dinner plate.

During an astonishing period from 1978 to 1980, Monsieur Mangetout took on an incredible challenge: to eat an entire Cessna 150 airplane. Yes, you read that correctly—a whole airplane! While other stories might involve eating smaller objects, Lotito aimed for something much grander in scale. With unwavering determination, he embarked on this monumental task.

Over the span of two years, Monsieur Mangetout steadily worked his way through the metal aircraft, taking it apart piece by piece. This wasn't something he accomplished in a single sitting; it required patience and resilience. Day by day, he inched closer to his unconventional goal, ultimately achieving what many thought impossible.

While the notion of eating an airplane might sound outlandish, there's an intriguing connection to our everyday relationship with food. While we're not dining on an aircraft, our eating habits often reflect Monsieur Mangetout's incredible feat in their sheer volume. Food is an integral part of our lives, offering both challenges and opportunities for exploration.

The Many Faces of Food

Food is not just sustenance; it's a profound part of our human experience. It's a social glue that binds us together, broadening our horizons and introducing us to diverse traditions. It's the soothing balm for the bereaved and the unifying force that brings us together in times of both joy and crisis.

Food is also remarkably polarizing. We judge others based on their diet, weight, and even table manners. The seemingly simple questions like, "Do you like pineapple on pizza?" or "Do you put sugar in your tea?" can reveal more about a person than you might think.

Our relationship with food is a time-consuming one. When you factor in food shopping, cooking, eating, and cleaning up the kitchen, we dedicate a significant portion of our lives—two whole months every year—to nourishing our bodies. It's a testament to the importance of food in our daily routines.

The Alarming Issue of Food Waste

However, as we consume this abundance of food, we must also confront the sobering issue of food waste. In the United States alone, households waste about a third of the food they purchase each year. It's not just a matter of financial waste but a matter of environmental concern.

The good news is that we have the power to reduce both the time and money spent on food while curbing waste through better planning and execution. This book is here to guide you through this journey. While it does include some recipes, it's not intended as a cookbook. Instead, it's meant to be your trusted companion for navigating the supermarket aisles and the labyrinth of your kitchen.

The Path to Efficiency

Boiled down to the essentials, you'll discover the only 10 kitchen tools you'll ever need, 10 food staples that will upgrade your kitchen game, and 10 dishes that will form the foundation of your personal repertoire. These are the building blocks that could lead to a great culinary career, facilitate a transition into a downsized life, or become a lifesaver for harried college students or anyone looking to streamline their meal planning.

Whether you're moving to a smaller kitchen, managing with a leaner budget, or simply desiring to eliminate the fuss from your daily life, this book is for you. It's a friendly guide aimed at helping you become more self-sufficient in the kitchen, make informed choices about your food, and reduce waste along the way.

So, as you undertake this culinary adventure, remember that food is more than just sustenance; it's a connector, a culture, and a canvas for creativity. Let's explore this world together, and may your kitchen become a place where you not only nourish your body but also your soul.

Chapter 2
Resourceful Cooking

Timeless and Global Traditions

Welcome to Chapter 2 of your kitchen guide, where we explore the art of simple, affordable cooking - a style of cuisine that has many names, but let's call it "resourceful cooking." In this chapter, we'll dive into this wonderful world of resourceful cooking, where simplicity meets creativity, and affordability doesn't mean sacrificing flavor or nutrition.

A Trend or a Necessity – It Doesn't Matter

Food trends come and go, but there's something timeless and universally appealing about resourceful cooking. This style of cuisine transcends boundaries, evolving over time and across geographical and socio-economic realms. It's a reminder that delicious, fulfilling meals can be created from humble ingredients without breaking the bank.

For some, resourceful cooking may be a necessity, a means of making ends meet. For others, it's an eco-adventure, a conscious choice to reduce waste, minimize environmental impact, and celebrate the bounty of nature. Whether you find yourself foraging for ingredients out of need or embracing it as an eco-friendly journey, resourceful cooking has something to offer.

The Richness of Poverty Cuisine

Resourceful cooking, often referred to as "poverty cuisine", is a fascinating tapestry of culinary traditions that varies widely depending on cultural and regional factors. It may involve basic ingredients such as rice, beans, potatoes, cheap cuts of meat, and seasonal vegetables. What's remarkable is how these ingredients are transformed into dishes that delight the taste buds and nourish the body, all while staying within budget.

A perfect example of Poverty Cuisine is "rice and beans": staples in many cuisines around the world. They are nutritional powerhouses that have sustained communities for centuries. Rich in protein, fiber, and essential nutrients, this dynamic duo forms the foundation of countless budget-friendly and nutritious meals. From Latin America to Asia, and beyond, rice and beans hold deep cultural significance, symbolizing resilience, resourcefulness, and community. Incorporating rice and beans into your diet not only ensures a balanced and wholesome meal but also honors a tradition of sustenance that transcends borders and generations.

Celebrating Resourcefulness

While resourceful cooking often originates from necessity and economic constraints, it's also a way to celebrate it - a testament to our ability to adapt, innovate, and make the most out of what we have. In today's world of endless choices and convenience, resourceful cooking reminds us of the beauty of simplicity and the satisfaction of creating a meal from scratch.

As you start your culinary journey as independent adults, we invite you to embrace the beauty of this cooking style. Whether you find yourself drawn to it out of need or as a conscious choice, remember that resourcefulness is a valuable skill that can serve you well in the kitchen and in life.

Resourceful cooking is not just about saving money; it's about savoring the joy of creating something delicious, nutritious, and sustainable. It's a reminder that the most memorable meals are often the simplest ones, crafted with love and care.

Applying Resourceful Cooking in your Everyday Life

Applying resourceful cooking techniques is all about making the most of what you already have at your disposal. Start by taking inventory of your pantry and fridge, prioritizing ingredients that are nearing their expiration dates. Get creative with your side dishes by exploring what's hiding in your pantry shelves. And when all else fails, don't hesitate to take advantage of supermarket sales to round out your meals.

Here's a practical example: imagine you find a head of broccoli on the brink of wilting, but still salvageable. Simply steam it for a quick and nutritious dish. Pair it with a forgotten slice of bread, perhaps the end piece, for a satisfying open-face sandwich. Need protein? Hard boil an egg or crack open a can of tuna. With a dash of seasoning and a little flair in presentation, you've crafted a vibrant and nourishing meal without spending a penny. After all, who's to say that the beloved "avocado toast" didn't originate from an ingenious college student looking to make the most of their limited ingredients?

Chapter 3

Kitchen Kickstart

10 Tools to Launch Your Culinary Adventure

Starting a new kitchen can be a thrilling yet somewhat overwhelming experience, especially when you're stepping into the world of independent adulthood. In this chapter, we'll introduce you to the essential tools you'll need to kickstart your cooking adventure. These tools are the backbone of your kitchen, designed to make your cooking endeavors efficient, versatile, and, most importantly, enjoyable.

Preparing for Your Culinary Voyage
As you open the door to your new kitchen, we assume that you already have some basics in place - a few pots and pans, some dishware, and a couple of forks. This book is your introductory guide to the world of food preparation and cooking. But before we dive into the heart of the kitchen, let's take stock of what you should already have:

The Refrigerator (or Ice Chest)
First and foremost, ensure you have a refrigerator or ice chest of some sort. This essential appliance will keep your ingredients fresh, your leftovers safe, and your beverages cool. It's the trusty guardian of your culinary treasures.

A Cooking Appliance

While we'll explore specific options in a later chapter, it's important to have at least one reliable cooking appliance in your kitchen. This is crucial for preparing meals and making your space truly functional. Don't worry, we'll dive deeper into the exciting world of cooking methods and equipment soon!

The Myth of Kitchen Gadgets

In a world where social media ads and late-night infomercials bombard you with flashy kitchen gadgets, it's easy to get swept away by the promise of convenience. However, we're here to set the record straight: you don't need a cluttered collection of gadgets to create culinary wonders. What you need are ten essential tools - solid, dependable instruments that will serve you well in a multitude of culinary tasks.

The Power of Multitasking

Your core kitchen should be designed for multitasking. These tools are carefully selected to help you perform various functions without the need for an overwhelming number of specialized gadgets. In essence, they help you cook efficiently and reduce the number of dirty dishes waiting for you post-meal.

The Art of Cleaning as You Go

Speaking of post-meal chores, here's a valuable tip: learn to clean as you go. It's a simple yet effective practice that will prevent a mountain of dirty dishes from taunting you after a satisfying meal. By keeping your workspace tidy and washing tools as you use them, you'll make the entire cooking experience smoother and more enjoyable.

Investing in Your Kitchen

Now, you might be wondering about the cost. Building a fully equipped kitchen doesn't have to break the bank. You can expect to spend less than $250 on the "Basic 10", and it's an investment well worth making. While you could spend less in the short run by opting for plastic instead of glass, we strongly recommend considering glass containers. They may have a slightly higher upfront cost, but they offer unparalleled versatility.

In the following sections, we'll introduce you to each of the "Basic 10" tools and explain why they are the cornerstone of any well-equipped kitchen. For the comprehensive list of kitchen tools mentioned in this guide, simply drop us an email at resources@introtofood.com, and we'll gladly provide you with online links to each item.

In our essential tools list, you'll find a variety of items to make your cooking journey smooth and enjoyable. While the best measurements often come from the heart, having the right tools can ensure your recipes turn out just right. Measuring spoons are essential for those moments when precision is key. Alongside these, a Pyrex measuring cup is invaluable, especially for liquids, acting as a trusted sidekick in your kitchen. For those who appreciate exactness, a kitchen scale can be your secret weapon, providing pinpoint accuracy as you gain confidence in the kitchen. Whether you're measuring with your heart or with precision, the joy of cooking and the satisfaction of creating delicious meals never waver. It's all about finding your own flavor and making magic happen in the kitchen!

Tool #1 - The Multifaceted Salad Spinner
Now, let's talk about one of the unsung heroes of your kitchen arsenal - the salad spinner. This unassuming tool is a true workhorse, and you'll soon discover it's much more than just a gadget for drying lettuce

INTRO TO FOOD ~ 13

A Salad Spinner's Hidden Talents
When choosing a salad spinner, opt for the kind with a separate basket, and you'll unlock a world of kitchen convenience. With this versatile tool, you'll not only get a large bowl but also a basket that doubles as a strainer. Plus, the pure, unbridled joy of dry lettuce awaits you!

Your Produce's Best Friend
One of the primary uses of a salad spinner is, of course, for its namesake - making crisp, dry salads. But it's not limited to just greens. You can utilize your salad spinner to wash all your produce effectively. Here's how:

Prep Your Produce: Start by placing your fruits or veggies in the basketless bowl.

Add Some Baking Soda: For a thorough clean, add a pinch of baking soda to the mix. It works wonders in removing impurities.

Cover with Water: Fill the bowl with water until your produce is comfortably submerged.

Swish and Soak: Gently swish the produce around with your hand, allowing the baking soda and water to work their magic. This step helps dislodge any dirt or contaminants.

Drain the Dirt: Once you're satisfied that your produce is squeaky clean, lift it out of the bowl. The dirt and impurities will stay behind in the water.

Time to Spin: For larger items like tomatoes or apples, a good drain is usually sufficient. However, for leafy greens, it's time to spin!

Spin Away: Place the basket filled with your drained leaves in the empty bowl, secure the lid on top, and start spinning. The centrifugal force will whisk away excess water, leaving your greens perfectly dry and ready for salad greatness.

But here's the fun part - your salad spinner isn't limited to the realm of the kitchen alone. In a pinch, it can even come to your rescue for tasks beyond the culinary world.

Spin Cycle: The Surprising Double Life of Your Salad Spinner!

So, here's a little secret we heard through the grapevine - apparently, a salad spinner isn't just for leafy greens anymore! In a pinch, some creative souls have been known to repurpose this kitchen gadget for, wait for it... laundry duty! Yep, you read that right.

Picture this: you're down to your last clean pair of socks, and the laundry room is a trek away. What's a busy student to do? Well, rumor has it that a salad spinner can come to the rescue. Just toss those socks in, give 'em a spin, and voilà - laundry day just got a whole lot easier! Now, we can't vouch for the effectiveness or longevity of this laundry hack, but hey, desperate times call for desperate measures, right?

Who knew your salad spinner could moonlight as a mini washing machine? Just be sure to give it a thorough clean before tossing your greens in there next time!

Tool #2 - A Manual Citrus Juicer

A manual citrus juicer is a true kitchen essential for a multitude of reasons. Firstly, it opens a world of flavor possibilities with its ability to extract fresh citrus juice effortlessly. Whether you're crafting refreshing mocktails, whisking up zesty salad dressings, or marinating meats with a tangy twist, citrus juice adds brightness and depth to any dish.

But wait, there's more! Beyond its culinary applications, citrus juice, particularly lemon juice, doubles as a handy cleaning agent. Its natural acidity makes it a powerful degreaser, perfect for tackling stubborn stains or cutting through grease in a pinch. So, not only does a manual citrus juicer refine your cooking endeavors, but it also lends a helping hand in keeping your kitchen sparkling clean.

Keep your kitchen organized with tools and ingredients easily accessible. An organized kitchen makes cooking more efficient and enjoyable.

And let's not forget the simplicity and ease of use that a manual citrus juicer offers. Unlike electric juicers, manual citrus juicers are typically compact, easy to clean, and don't require electricity, making them perfect for small kitchens or dorm rooms. Additionally, the process of manually squeezing citrus fruits can be quite therapeutic and satisfying, adding a touch of joy to your cooking experience. These aspects further highlight why a manual citrus juicer is an indispensable kitchen tool for any budding chef.

Tool #3 - A Large, Graduated Glass Bowl with Vented Lid

Glass is your ideal ally in the world of food preparation. Imagine having a versatile large glass container with a vented lid at your disposal; it's like having a magician's hat in your kitchen. This remarkable tool isn't just a bowl; it's your ticket to culinary convenience and precision.

Versatile Microwave Cooking

When it's time to whip up a quick meal, your large glass container steps up to the plate. Its microwave-friendly design makes it a versatile tool for cooking pasta to perfection or steaming a medley of vegetables with ease. And if you don't have a microwave yet, you can easily pick one up for under $100, opening a world of convenient cooking options. Plus, that vented lid? It's your secret weapon for controlled cooking, ensuring your dishes turn out just right, every time.

Precision in Every Recipe

Picture this: you're following a recipe, and precision is key. The etched measurements on your trusty glass container come to your rescue. No more guessing or searching for the right measuring cup; it's all right there, etched on the glass, ensuring your dishes are as close to the recipe as can be.

Your All-in-One Workhorse

But that's not all. Your large glass vessel is not limited to one task: it's a multitasking marvel. Whether you're measuring ingredients, mixing up a batter, cooking up a storm, prepping your ingredients, or elegantly serving a dish, this glass wonder does it all. It seamlessly transitions from one role to another, making your kitchen endeavors smoother and more enjoyable.

In the world of kitchen essentials, your large glass bowl with a vented lid is a true game-changer. It's not just a tool; it's a culinary companion, ready to assist you in your gastronomic adventures. So, as you launch your culinary journey, remember that this glass wonder is here to make your life in the kitchen simpler.

Tool #4 - A Manual Can Opener

Let's talk about an indispensable tool in your kitchen arsenal - the manual can opener. Now, you might have noticed that some cans come with convenient pull tabs, but here's the deal: those pull tabs can make the canned goods a bit pricier.

However, there's more to the story.
Beyond the budget-friendly aspect, a manual can opener serves another crucial purpose - it's your lifeline in emergencies or natural disasters. Imagine a situation where the power is out, and you're left with canned food as your only source of sustenance. In times like these, a manual can opener becomes your reliable ally, allowing you to access your canned goods without relying on electricity. It's a small yet vital tool that ensures you're prepared for the unexpected, making it an essential addition to your kitchen toolkit.

Tool #5 - Glass Food Storage with Lids – Assorted Sizes

Now, let's talk about a kitchen essential that not only offers practical advantages but also adds a touch of elegance to your culinary journey - glass food storage with lids. While we could sing praises about its proprietary benefits, let's focus on why it's simply the best choice for your kitchen.

The Allure of Glass
First and foremost, there's something inherently appealing

about glass. It exudes a sense of quality and transparency that you'll come to appreciate. Unlike other materials, glass doesn't absorb odors or colors from your food, ensuring that your meals always taste as they should.

From Fridge to Table
One of the remarkable features of glass containers is their versatility. An unappetizing leftover may find its way to the trash in other containers, but with glass, your creations travel seamlessly from the fridge to the microwave, and finally, to the table with grace and style. It's a small but significant detail that improves your dining experience.

Endless Possibilities
When it comes to glass food storage, you have plenty of options. You can wash and reuse empty food jars, contributing to sustainability while saving money. Alternatively, you can explore assorted sets with colorful lids that not only keep your food fresh but also add a pop of personality to your kitchen. And let's not forget about the classic mason jars, available in a multitude of sizes, perfect for preserving jams, pickles, or simply showcasing your creations.

Incorporating glass food storage into your kitchen not only enriches the practicality of your food storage but also brings a touch of sophistication to your culinary endeavors. So, whether you're storing leftovers or presenting your latest masterpiece at the dining table, remember that with glass, you're not just preserving food; you're preserving an aesthetic that boosts your kitchen experience.

Tool #6 - A Knife Set
A reliable set of knives is a must-have in your kitchen toolkit, and you don't need an array of specialty blades to get started. Opt for a basic knife set that includes essential knives like a chef's knife, a paring knife, and a serrated knife. Choose knives that feel comfortable in your hand and are versatile enough to handle a variety of tasks.

Keeping your knives clean and dry is essential for their longevity, but avoid putting them in the dishwasher as it can damage the blades over time. To store them safely, consider investing in a knife block or magnetic strip to keep them organized and easily accessible. Some budget-friendly knife sets even come with their own protective sheaths, allowing you to store them securely in a drawer or take them on the go.

Tool #7 - Cutting Boards
When it comes to cutting boards, the choice between wood and plastic is entirely yours to make. Both options have their unique advantages, and the decision depends on your personal preferences.

A beautifully crafted wood cutting board, for instance, can serve a dual purpose. Not only is it a practical tool for food preparation, but it can also double as an elegant display or serving dish for shared appetizers or charcuterie. Picture arranging a colorful array of cheeses, fruits, and savory bites on a rustic wooden board – it's not just functional; it's a work of culinary art.

On the other hand, plastic cutting boards come in a vast array of colors, shapes, sizes, and thicknesses, allowing you to choose one that suits your style and needs perfectly.

Now, here's a practical tip: consider getting at least three cutting boards and assign a specific role to each:

The Aromatic Ally
Some ingredients, like onions and garlic, leave behind lingering smells that can affect the flavors of other foods. To avoid unexpectedly garlicky apples or onion-flavored cucumbers, designate one cutting board for these aromatic ingredients.

The Fresh and Fabulous
Fresh produce, from vibrant veggies to juicy fruits, deserves their own dedicated cutting board. This ensures that your fruits and vegetables retain their crispness and natural flavors without any traces of the previous night's garlic.

The Meat Maestro
When it comes to handling meats, safety is paramount. Using a separate cutting board exclusively for meats helps prevent cross-contamination. Raw meat can harbor harmful bacteria, and keeping it away from foods intended to be consumed raw is a crucial step in ensuring food safety.

By having these three cutting boards at your disposal, you'll streamline your cooking process while maintaining the highest standards of food hygiene. Plus, it adds a touch of organization and efficiency to your kitchen routine, making the journey even more enjoyable.

Tool #8 – *Pyrex Measuring Cups*
Pyrex measuring cups are an essential tool in any kitchen for several reasons. Firstly, their durable glass construction makes them resistant to heat, which means you can use them for both hot and cold ingredients without worrying about warping or damage. Additionally, the clear markings on the cups make it easy to accurately measure ingredients, ensuring precise results in your cooking and baking endeavors. Pyrex measuring cups are also versatile; you can use them in the microwave, refrigerator, freezer, and dishwasher, making them incredibly convenient for a wide range of tasks. Plus, their sturdy handles and spouts make pouring and transferring liquids a breeze. With Pyrex measuring cups in your kitchen arsenal, you'll be equipped to tackle any recipe with confidence and precision.

Tool #9 - *An Immersion Blender with Whisk Attachment*
A true kitchen multitasker, the immersion blender is your ticket to versatility. With this handy tool, you can transform ordinary ingredients into extraordinary creations. Here are just a few of the culinary feats you can achieve with it:

Soups and Smoothies
Leftover vegetables can be magically turned into hearty soups, while fruits become vibrant and restorative smoothies.

Salad Dressings
Thanks to the whisk attachment, you'll effortlessly emulsify olive oil and lemon juice, creating healthy and light salad dressings that elevate your greens.

Velvety Textures
Say goodbye to lumpy mashed potatoes (or cauliflower) and

cake batter. With the immersion blender, both will take on a velvety, smooth texture that's simply irresistible.

Whipped Delights

Watch heavy cream transform into a fluffy, dreamy dessert topping, perfect for sundaes or pies. You can also turn egg whites into airy meringue for delicate confections.

Chickpea Magic

Instead of letting the viscous liquid from canned chickpeas go down the sink, use your immersion blender to whisk it into a thick foam. It's a fantastic vegan alternative to egg whites in recipes.

But here's the best part: an immersion blender can accomplish all of this without the need for a countertop container blender or a handheld mixer. It's not only a space-saving wonder but also a budget-friendly alternative that empowers you to explore your creativity to the fullest. With this tool by your side, your kitchen adventures are about to reach new heights!

Tool #10 - A Vegetable Peeler

Let's talk about one of the kitchen essentials that will become your trusty sidekick - the vegetable peeler. This handy tool is a game-changer when it comes to efficiency and minimizing waste in the kitchen. Its primary purpose is to make the peeling process quick and easy, far more so than struggling with a knife. But the magic of a vegetable peeler doesn't stop there. It shines when you're working with fruits and vegetables that have thin or delicate skin, like apples, pears, cucumbers, carrots, and potatoes. Beyond the basics, a vegetable peeler has a hidden talent - it can also zest lemons, adding a burst of citrusy flavor to your dishes with ease. So, get ready to welcome this versatile tool into your kitchen, and you'll wonder how you ever prepared food without it!

Chapter 4
Invest in Quality

The Value of Premium Ingredients

Did you know that a moderate grocery budget amounts to $400 per month per person, and that's solely for groceries, excluding take-out or dining out? Surprisingly, despite the investment in ingredients, approximately one-third - a whopping $120 - goes to waste. It's here that home cooking becomes not just a matter of practicality but a delightful adventure with financial rewards.

The Power of Quality Ingredients
Have you ever wondered if a $20 piece of artisanal cheese tastes significantly better than a $5 mass-produced block? The truth is, it's a matter of personal preference, and price doesn't always equate to taste. However, there's a gourmet truth that we stand by: a $3 box of pasta can deliver flavors and satisfaction that far surpass its $1 counterpart. When it comes to your kitchen, splurge is in the eye of the beholder and the size and of their pocketbook.

The Essentials and Splurge-Worthy Staples
In this chapter, we'll introduce you to 10 kitchen essentials and splurge-worthy staples that will make a noticeable difference in your cooking adventures. Each of these ingredients serves a purpose beyond filling your pantry. They are carefully selected to refine your dishes, add depth to your flavors, and boost your epicurean experiences.

Building Confidence and Efficiency

With these essentials in your kitchen, you're not just cooking; you're crafting delightful, memorable dishes that reflect your unique taste and style. Having a well-stocked pantry instills confidence in the kitchen. You'll be better prepared to tackle recipes, experiment with flavors, and improvise when you need to. These staples offer versatility, allowing you to plan meals efficiently and reduce waste.

A Frugal Approach with Long-Term Benefits

You'll soon discover that acquiring these staples is not just about survival but about enjoying the art of cooking. It's about creating delicious meals that suit your tastes while making a frugal yet forward-thinking investment. Choosing quality ingredients over cheap alternatives can be a smart financial move in the long run, as these staples can be used in countless dishes, saving you both time and money.

A Healthier You

Lastly, it's worth noting that many of these staples come with health benefits, contributing to a balanced and nutritious diet. They provide the foundation for meals that nourish your body and mind, promoting overall well-being.

So, let's dive into this food exploration together. These 10 staples are more than just ingredients; they are the building blocks of culinary artistry. Get ready to discover the magic they bring to your cooking and the joy they add to your dining table. Your kitchen is about to become the canvas for a gastronomic masterpiece, and we're here to guide you every step of the way.

Staple #1 - Fresh Lemons

Let's talk about one of the essential staples that will brighten up your kitchen: fresh lemons. Bottled lemon juice may be convenient, but it pales in comparison to the real deal. Fresh lemons bring a unique flavor, zesty brightness, and incredible versatility that will truly boost your epicurean game.

The Zesty Magic of Fresh Lemons

Fresh lemons are a culinary powerhouse. Their vibrant acidity can work wonders in your kitchen. For starters, the acidity in lemon juice can be your secret weapon when it comes to tenderizing meat and seafood in marinades. It not only infuses a delightful tang but also helps break down the fibers, leaving you with perfectly succulent dishes.

Keeping Freshness Intact

Lemons also play a crucial role in preserving the freshness of certain fruits. When you sprinkle or drizzle a bit of lemon juice on fruits like apples and avocados, it acts as a natural shield against browning due to oxidation. This not only keeps your salads and snacks looking enticing but also improves their flavor profiles.

The Heart of Salad Dressings

In the world of salad dressings, lemon juice is a superstar. Its bright, citrusy notes add a refreshing twist to any dressing, elevating your salads from ordinary to extraordinary. A simple blend of olive oil, lemon juice, and a pinch of salt and pepper can turn a bowl of greens into a gourmet delight.

The Versatile Trio: Juice, Zest, and Slices

What makes fresh lemons truly invaluable are their various forms of culinary expression. You have the lemon juice, which can be used in marinades, dressings, and beverages, infusing a burst of flavor wherever it goes. Then there's the zest, the finely grated outer peel, which is a treasure trove of aromatic oils, perfect for adding depth and fragrance to both sweet and savory dishes. And let's not forget about lemon slices, which serve as a beautiful garnish for drinks, a refreshing addition to water, or a flavorful companion to a variety of dishes.

Your Culinary Companion
In your journey toward sustenance independence, fresh lemons will be an essential ingredient. Their versatility, flavor, and ability to transform dishes and drinks make them an essential addition to your kitchen. Whether you're exploring new recipes, experimenting with flavors, or simply brightening up your everyday meals, fresh lemons are your ticket to creating a wide range of delicious culinary delights. So, welcome them into your kitchen, and let the zestiness begin!

Staple #2 - Bouillon/Broth
In any kitchen, whether you're a seasoned chef or just starting out, bouillon or broth is an absolute essential. But here's the thing: not all bouillon is created equal. When it comes to flavor, you want the good stuff – not just a salty cube. Investing in the best quality bouillon or broth can truly make a world of difference in your cooking. Think rich, complex flavors that enrich your soups, stews, and sauces to new heights. We swear by a jarred product called "Better Than Bouillon" available in chicken, beef, pork, vegetables, and many other flavors! When it comes to bouillon and broth, don't be afraid to splurge a little. Trust us, your taste buds will thank you!

A Warm Hug on a Cold Day
Imagine a cold, wintry day, and you're craving something warm

and comforting. A cup of bouillon can be your quick fix for warmth and coziness. Simply spoon some paste into hot water, and you have a steaming cup of savory delight to ward off the chill.

The Foundation of Hearty Meals
With bouillon, you can effortlessly transform everyday ingredients into hearty and satisfying meals. For instance, if you have a handful of frozen vegetables and some bouillon on hand, you're just minutes away from a delicious homemade soup. It's the kind of kitchen magic that turns a simple collection of ingredients into a bowl of warmth and nourishment.

Elevating the Humble Grain
Another ingenious use of bouillon is to swap it in for plain water when cooking rice, quinoa, or other whole grains. This simple substitution can turn an otherwise mundane side dish into a flavorful and substantial meal base. It's a fantastic way to infuse grains with a rich, savory essence that pairs beautifully with various proteins and vegetables.

Your Flavorful Ally
As you venture on your journey into the world of independent adulthood, bouillon will be your flavorful ally in the kitchen. Its versatility, ability to enrich the taste of countless dishes, and the warmth it brings to your heart on those chilly days make it an indispensable staple. So, keep bouillon in your pantry or refrigerator, and you'll always have a reliable secret ingredient to transform your inner chef's creations into savory delights.

Staple #3 - Grinding Pepper

When it comes to pepper, freshly ground is the way to go. While the pre-ground version has its place, there are distinct advantages to opting for whole peppercorns and grinding them yourself, especially as you become more immersed in cooking.

A Mill You Can Fill
As you delve deeper into your cooking adventures, you might find that pre-filled grinders have limitations. They are often single-use and can't be refilled, which can be both wasteful and limiting in the long run. This is where a pepper mill that you can fill with whole peppercorns comes into play.

Preserving Essential Oils and Flavor
The magic of freshly ground pepper lies in its ability to preserve essential oils and volatile compounds, which are responsible for its distinct aroma and flavor. Unlike pre-ground pepper, which may lose some of these precious components over time, freshly ground pepper offers a burst of bold, aromatic goodness that can transform your dishes.

Tailored Heat for Your Plates
Another advantage of having a pepper mill at your disposal is the ability to customize the level of subtle bite for each plate. Whether you prefer a nuanced sprinkle or a hearty dash of pep-

per, having a pepper grinder allows you to season your dishes precisely to your liking.

Your Culinary Companion

As you navigate the realm of independent cooking, consider adding a pepper mill filled with whole peppercorns to your kitchen arsenal. It's a small yet impactful investment that will upgrade your culinary creations by infusing them with the vibrant flavors and aromas of freshly ground pepper. So, let your taste buds savor the difference, and keep a pepper grinder on hand to add that perfect dash of picante to your dishes.

Staple #4 - Table Salt

Also known as refined salt or common salt, it's a versatile seasoning that's essential for most seasoning purposes. But there's more to it than just flavor; it also plays a crucial role in supporting your body's health.

The Everyday Seasoning

Table salt is the go-to salt for your cooking adventures. Whether you're sprinkling a pinch to improve the taste of your favorite dishes or precisely measuring it in recipes, it's the culinary staple that adds that familiar, satisfying saltiness.

Iodine: A Vital Trace Element

Here's an important aspect of table salt that you may not be aware of: iodine. Iodine is an essential trace element that your body needs for the proper functioning of the thyroid gland, which plays a pivotal role in maintaining your overall health. To ensure you get your required daily intake of iodine, it's wise to choose salt labeled as "iodized." This simple choice can go a long way in supporting your well-being.

The Bouillon and Broth Consideration
One important factor to keep in mind: when using bouillon or broth in your cooking, remember that these ingredients are naturally salty. Because of their savory essence, you may discover that you don't need to incorporate additional salt into your dishes. Achieving the perfect balance of flavors is key, and experimenting with your seasoning will enhance your culinary skills.

Staple #5 - Good Pasta – The Best You Can Afford
While it's known as a budget-friendly option, there's a world of variety and quality waiting to be discovered when it comes to this beloved pantry staple.

The Luxury of Premium Pasta
While budget-friendly pasta is readily available, it's worth mentioning that there's a world of high-end pasta brands that offer a different culinary experience. These premium pasta brands often use higher-quality durum wheat semolina flour, resulting in a superior texture and flavor. The production methods for premium pasta are equally important, with some brands employing traditional techniques like bronze die extrusion or slow drying. These methods can leave the pasta with a slightly rougher surface texture, which is ideal for holding onto sauce, creating a more satisfying eating experience.

A Matter of Personal Taste
Ultimately, your choice of pasta comes down to personal taste. Whether you opt for budget-friendly varieties or indulge in premium options, pasta is a canvas for your creativity in the kitchen. Different shapes and brands can add delightful twists to your recipes, making your meals exciting and enjoyable.

Your Culinary Canvas
Pasta is not just a pantry staple; it's a culinary canvas waiting to be adorned with your creativity. Whether you opt for the simplicity of budget-friendly pasta or the luxury of premium varieties, enjoy the process of discovering new flavors and textures. Your kitchen is your playground, and pasta is your versatile companion on this delicious adventure. So, have fun experimenting with different brands and shapes, and savor every bite of your budget-friendly kitchen thrill!

Staple #6 - Garlic

Often sold as a whole bulb, cloaked in papery white skin, garlic is a culinary treasure with multiple layers of both flavor and versatility.

Unlocking the Garlic Bulb
A garlic bulb, also referred to as a "head" of garlic, is a cluster of individual lobes connected to a central root. These individual lobes, known as cloves, are the prized gems of garlic, each holding the promise of aromatic richness.

A Flavorful Powerhouse
Garlic's reputation as a kitchen staple is well-deserved, thanks to its robust and distinctive flavor. It has the remarkable ability to infuse depth and complexity into a wide spectrum of dishes. Its profile is a symphony of savory, slightly spicy, and subtly sweet notes, capable of enhancing the taste of countless recipes.

The Aroma of Freshness
Fresh garlic is not only a culinary powerhouse but also a budget-friendly addition to your kitchen. It's easily accessible and a cinch to prepare. To peel a clove, place it on a cutting board and give it a gentle smash with the flat side of a knife. The skin

will quickly separate from the flesh, leaving you with a fragrant, ready-to-use ingredient.

Convenience in a Jar
For added convenience, you can find ready-to-use minced garlic in squeeze jars. While purists may argue that fresh is best, these jars offer a quick and easy alternative when you're pressed for time or simply looking to streamline your cooking process.

Your Flavorful Ally
As you venture into the world of independent cooking, garlic will be your flavorful ally in the kitchen. It's not just an ingredient; it's a key to unlocking a world of taste possibilities. From aromatic sautés to rich sauces and marinades, garlic has your back. So, whether you choose to work with fresh cloves or opt for the convenience of minced garlic, embrace the aromatic richness it brings to your creations.

Staple #7 - Baking Soda
Let's explore one of the kitchen essentials that's not only budget-friendly but also incredibly versatile – baking soda. This humble 8-ounce box, often costing around a dollar, is a true magician in your kitchen.

A Multi-Purpose Wonder
Baking soda is your kitchen's Swiss Army knife, capable of a wide range of tasks. Its versatility is matched only by its affordability, making it a must-have in your pantry.

Banishing Unwanted Odors
Ever wondered how to bid farewell to those pesky food odors lingering in your refrigerator? Baking soda is the answer. Simply leave an open box in your fridge, and it will dutifully absorb and

neutralize those unwanted scents, keeping your food smelling fresh.

Produce Saver

When it comes to cleaning your fruits and vegetables, baking soda is a fantastic ally. A tablespoon of baking soda added to a bowl of water transforms into a terrific produce cleaner. This simple solution helps remove dirt, pesticides, and residues, ensuring your produce is not only clean but also safe to eat.

The Stain Whisperer

Stubborn stains and burnt-on residues on your pots, pans, and baking sheets don't stand a chance against baking soda's cleaning prowess. Sprinkle it on the affected areas, add some hot water, and let it soak. After a brief hiatus, give it a good scrub, and you'll be amazed at how easily those stains vanish.

DIY Household Cleaner

Baking soda isn't limited to your kitchen; it's a star ingredient in many DIY household cleaners. By mixing it with water, you can create a versatile paste ideal for scrubbing and cleaning various surfaces. From countertops and stovetops to sinks, baking soda is your trusted partner in keeping your living spaces sparkling clean.

Your Budget-Friendly Companion

Throughout your culinary journey, keep baking soda on your list of essential pantry staples. Its versatility extends far beyond baking, making it an invaluable asset in your kitchen and your home. With a box of baking soda at your disposal, you're armed with a powerful and budget-friendly companion ready to tackle kitchen odors, produce cleaning, stain removal, and household cleaning. Embrace the magic of baking soda and let it simplify your daily life.

Staple #8 - The Essential Oils: Extra Virgin and Pure Olive Oils

In the bustling world of the kitchen, there are few ingredients as versatile and essential as olive oil. If you're just starting out, let's dive into why having not one, but two different types of olive oil in your pantry can take your cooking game to new heights.

EVOO

First up, we have extra virgin olive oil (EVOO for short). This golden elixir is the cream of the crop, prized for its superior quality and rich, nutty flavor profile. Perfect for drizzling over salads, dipping crusty bread, or finishing off a dish, extra virgin olive oil adds a luxurious touch to any culinary creation. Its delicate flavor and low smoke point make it ideal for dressings, marinades, and light sautéing, allowing the natural essence of your ingredients to shine through.

Pure Olive Oil

Now, let's turn our attention to pure olive oil. Don't let the name fool you – while it may not have the same cachet as its extra virgin counterpart, pure olive oil is a workhorse in the kitchen. With a milder flavor and higher smoke point, pure olive oil is your go-to for everyday cooking tasks like frying, roasting, and baking. Its neutral taste won't overpower your dishes, making it a versatile and reliable ally.

Smoke Point Consideration
But wait, there's more to olive oil than just flavor and application. Understanding smoke points is key to unlocking the full potential of these kitchen essentials. Extra virgin olive oil has a lower smoke point, which means it's best suited for low to medium heat cooking. Use EVOO for gently sautéing vegetables, aromatics, or seafood over low to medium heat to preserve its delicate flavor.

On the other hand, pure olive oil boasts a higher smoke point, making it better suited for high heat cooking methods like frying and roasting.

So, there you have it – the dynamic duo of extra virgin and pure olive oils. By having both varieties on hand, you'll be equipped to tackle any recipe that comes your way, from salads to stir-fries and everything in between. With a little bit of knowledge and a splash of olive oil, the possibilities are endless in your kitchen adventures.

Staple #9 - Dry Minimally-Processed Whole Grains

Whole grains take a bit more time to cook compared to their processed counterparts, but they offer a world of taste and health benefits that make the extra effort worthwhile.

The Wholesome Choice
In the world of grains, the least processed options often stand out as both the most affordable and the healthiest. They might require a bit of patience in the cooking process, but the rewards are well worth it. Whole grains, in their unadulterated form, retain their natural flavors and nutritional value.

Flavor Absorbers

One of the remarkable qualities of whole grains is their ability to absorb the flavors of the liquids they cook in. While following the cooking instructions on the package, consider substituting water with savory broth. This simple swap will infuse your grains with delicious depth, turning them into a delightful foundation for your meals.

Nutritional Powerhouses

Whole grains like brown rice, barley, quinoa, buckwheat, and farro are nutritional powerhouses. Unlike their processed counterparts, they contain all parts of the grain kernel, including the fiber-rich bran and nutrient-packed germ. This makes them rich in dietary fiber, which has numerous benefits for digestion, weight management, and heart health. By incorporating whole grains into your diet, you're not only satisfying your taste buds but also nourishing your body.

Versatile and Satisfying

Cooked whole grains can be enjoyed in various ways. You can savor them on their own, showcasing their natural goodness, or mix them with ingredients like chicken and vegetables to create hearty and wholesome dishes. The versatility of whole grains knows no bounds, making them a valuable addition to your kitchen.

Your Nutrient-Rich Foundation

Make whole grains a cornerstone of your pantry. Their affordability, nutritional richness, and flavor-absorbing abilities make them an excellent choice for budget-conscious and health-conscious cooks. With a bit of time management and creative cooking, you'll discover that whole grains are not just a kitchen staple but also a flavorful and nutritious foundation for countless culinary adventures.

Staple #10 - *Favorite Condiment*

Let's add a dash of flavor to your kitchen essentials with condiments. These flavor enhancers come in various forms, from ketchup and mustard to hot sauce and spicy mayo. The beauty of condiments lies in their ability to lift or rescue your culinary endeavors.

Your Flavorful Ally

In the world of cooking, we all have our favorite condiments. Whether it's the classic tang of ketchup, the zing of mustard, the fiery kick of hot sauce, or the creamy goodness of spicy mayo, the choice is entirely yours. Condiments are like culinary safety nets, ready to step in and save the day when your kitchen experiments take an unexpected turn.

A Tasty Lifesaver

Picture this: you've ventured into the world of independent cooking, trying out new recipes and techniques. But every now and then, a dish may not turn out exactly as you imagined. That's where your trusty condiments come into play. A dollop of ketchup, a drizzle of hot sauce, or a smear of spicy mayo can transform a less-than-perfect meal into a tasty triumph.

Versatile and Forgiving

Condiments are forgiving in nature. They blend effortlessly with a wide range of dishes, adding bursts of flavor and excitement. From dressing up burgers and sandwiches to elevating the simplest of snacks, condiments have the power to make your meals memorable.

Your Flavor Palette

Don't forget to stock up on your favorite condiment. It's not just a flavor enhancer; it's your versatile ally in the kitchen. So, whether you're creating culinary masterpieces or simply enjoying everyday meals, let your condiment of choice be your secret weapon. With it by your side, your kitchen adventures will always end on a flavorful note.

Chapter 5

Stretching the Shelf

Make Your Groceries Go the Distance

Navigating your grocery budget with savvy can turn the kitchen into a place of creativity rather than financial stress. It's about finding that sweet spot where you're not over-purchasing - leading to waste - but also ensuring you have enough staples on hand to pull together a nourishing meal at any time. While meal planning is a fantastic tool to keep your eating habits on track and your budget in check, life's spontaneity - like a surprise dinner invite - shouldn't throw a wrench into your plans or make you fret over the fate of your fridge's contents.

Shop Your Fridge and Pantry
Shop your fridge and pantry before heading to the store. Check for items nearing expiration and find creative ways to use them. That half-full jar of pasta sauce and lone can of beans can easily become a quick and delicious meal.

Portion Control
As you prepare your meals, keep portion control in mind. Understanding appropriate serving sizes not only helps prevent overeating but also reduces food waste. By serving yourself the right amount, you're less likely to have leftover food that goes uneaten or, worse, ends up in the trash.

Make Sure a Deal is Really a Deal

Supermarkets frequently release circulars or feature their latest deals on mobile apps, offering a treasure trove of savings. By basing your meal plans around what's on sale, you'll not only stretch your dollars further but also have the chance to experiment with new ingredients and recipes you might not have considered otherwise.

Buyer beware! It's tempting to grab every coupon and jump on every buy-one-get-one deal you come across. However, not all coupons and offers are created equal. Some might lead you to spend more on items you wouldn't have bought otherwise. Before using a coupon or taking advantage of an offer, ask yourself if it truly aligns with your meal plan and your budget. Sometimes, simplicity and sticking to your list are the best strategies for saving money.

Leftovers Strategy

Don't overlook the power of leftovers. Leftover food can be a valuable resource in your meal planning arsenal. Instead of letting them go to waste, consider how you can creatively repurpose them into new dishes. Last night's roasted vegetables make a delicious omelet filling for breakfast, and leftover grilled chicken is perfect on top of a salad for lunch. By incorporating leftovers into your meal planning, you reduce food waste, save time, and stretch your food budget.

Meal Prep and Batch Cooking

When time is scarce during the week, meal prep and batch cooking can be your saviors. Set aside some time on the weekend or during moments of free time to cook in larger quantities. Prepare meals that can be portioned and stored for later in the week. For instance, a big pot of chili can provide several dinners or lunches, saving you the hassle of cooking every day.

Budget Tracking

To stay within your budget and manage your grocery expenses effectively, consider keeping track of your spending. There are various apps and tools available that can help you monitor your purchases and identify areas where you can cut costs. Over time, you'll become more adept at making informed decisions about your grocery shopping.

Pantry Staples

Creating a well-stocked pantry is a cornerstone of successful meal planning. Simply use the *Essential Staples*, *First Grocery*, and *Beyond the Basics* shopping lists located in the Resources chapter.

There's a hidden pitfall you should watch out for - shopping while hungry. Picture this: you've just finished a grueling class or a long day of studying, and your stomach is growling louder than your professor's lecture. You rush to the grocery store with your shopping list in hand, but as you wander the aisles, your hunger-induced cravings can lead you astray.

In moments of ravenous hunger, you might be tempted to grab anything that looks appealing, often leading to impulse buys that derail your meal plan. Before you know it, you've got a bag of chips, a candy bar, or a fast-food meal deal in your cart - all because they seemed too good to pass up.

To combat this, consider a savvy strategy: buy something to eat right away before diving into your grocery shopping. For instance, you could grab a yogurt, a piece of fruit, or a snack bar. This immediate snack will only add a few minutes to your shopping trip, and will take the edge off your hunger and help you shop with a clear, focused mind. It can be the difference between sticking to your meal plan and succumbing to the allure of the fast-food drive-thru on the way home because you're too exhausted or famished to cook.

Flexible Meal Plans
Remember that meal planning doesn't have to be rigid. While having a plan is essential, it's also crucial to be flexible and adaptable. Sometimes, spontaneous meals can be just as satisfying as meticulously planned ones. Life happens, and being able to adjust your meal plan to fit your schedule and preferences will make the process more enjoyable. A handful of nuts, a cheese stick, a few crackers, and a carrot constitute a full meal. You may even call it a "charcuterie board"!

Cultural and Dietary Considerations
Incorporate your cultural background and dietary preferences into your meal planning. Consider any dietary restrictions, allergies, or cultural preferences when selecting recipes and ingredients. Meal planning is about creating meals that align with your personal needs and tastes, so don't be afraid to customize and experiment.

Waste Reduction
A responsible cook is also a mindful one. Minimizing food waste

is not only eco-friendly but also budget-friendly. Get creative with ingredients to use all parts effectively. Vegetable scraps can be turned into flavorful broths, and citrus zest can add a zing to your dishes. The less you waste, the more you save.

Community Resources

Explore local food resources that might offer affordable and fresh options. Farmers' markets, co-ops, and food-sharing initiatives can be excellent places to find high-quality produce and products while supporting your community.

Navigating the Aisles

As you wander the aisles of the supermarket, keep in mind that the placement of products is strategic. Companies pay a premium for their products to be displayed on end-caps, those shelves at the end of the aisles. While they may catch your eye, it doesn't necessarily mean they're the best value or quality. Often, the best deals are tucked away on the lower shelves, where high-quality products without hefty slotting fees are waiting to be discovered.

As you navigate the grocery store aisles, you'll encounter two distinct categories of food: perishable and non-perishable. Achieving a balance between these not only enriches your diet but also prepares you for the demands of your ever-changing schedule, from busy weeks filled with study sessions to spontaneous gatherings with friends. Let's delve into how to curate a pantry that supports both your health and your spontaneity, ensuring you're always ready for the next culinary adventure.

Non-Perishables: Mastering Canned Goods

Canned foods and other non-perishables are indispensable allies in the kitchen, boasting lengthy shelf lives without the need for refrigeration. This category includes not only canned goods but also staples like pasta, rice, beans, and grains. A quick inspection for rust around the seals of a can is wise before purchasing. While dented cans might be a bargain (and are generally safe), steer clear of any can showing signs of swelling, as it indicates spoilage.

A well-stocked pantry with a selection of canned proteins (such as tuna or chicken), vegetables (like corn or green beans), and beans (think chickpeas and kidney beans) ensures that you're never far from a nutritious meal. Imagine creating a vibrant salad with just these ingredients and a simple homemade dressing of olive oil, lemon juice, salt, and pepper. It's an affordable yet delicious way to dine.

When selecting cans, note that those with pull-up tabs might be pricier than their flat-lid cousins. Given that you'll need a can opener for many canned goods, opting for the regular cans could be more economical.

To drain or not to drain the liquid from canned foods? That's up to personal preference and the dish you're preparing. While the liquid in canned fish, packed in oil or water, and the syrup in canned fruits can add flavor or sweetness to your meals, you might want to drain canned vegetables to reduce salt intake. The starchy liquid from canned beans can thicken soups and stews if you choose to keep it.

Remember, once opened, the contents of a can become perishable. Transfer any leftovers to a lidded glass container (a handy item from your Startup Kit) to keep them fresh and prevent any transfer of odors or tastes from the can. This small step will ensure your opened non-perishables remain as delightful as when you first popped the seal.

Non-Perishables: The Convenience of Bagged and Boxed Foods

Bagged and boxed items hold a special place in the world of non-perishables. They're designed to outlast a single meal - though, let's face it, a quick ramen or mac-and-cheese dinner straight from the pot is a classic student experience. On days when you're not indulging in these instant comforts, take a moment to check if the packaging is resealable. This small step can significantly extend the freshness of your food and prevent unnecessary waste.

Before you tear into a box, look for a "tab and groove" closure that allows for easy resealing, preserving the contents for future use. Shopping with an eye for practical packaging can save you money in the long run, as extra frills often come with an added price tag.

Keeping your food safe from pests is crucial. Always inspect packaging for any openings that could invite unwanted guests, particularly those with a sweet tooth. For bags of grains, beans, or pasta, various household items can serve as makeshift seals—a chip clip, a clothespin, or even a sturdy rubber band from your stalks of broccoli can do the trick. While we've come across inventive solutions like using hair ties to seal chip bags, there are more straightforward approaches that might serve you better.

Decanting, or transferring food from its original packaging to a more durable container, is not just about keeping pests out; it also helps in organizing your pantry and keeping things neat. If you opt to decant, remember to save the cooking instructions. Snipping out the directions and placing them inside or attached to your new container ensures that you won't find yourself guessing how long to cook that brown rice. This approach not only protects your food but also turns your pantry into a model of efficiency and style, no matter its size.

Navigating the World of Perishables

Perishable foods, those that can spoil or decay, often require special attention, mainly refrigeration, to keep them fresh and safe to eat. Here's a straightforward guide to help you manage these essentials with care:

Mimic the Supermarket's Storage: An easy rule of thumb for storing perishable items is to replicate how they were stored at the grocery store. If you pick it up from a freezer, it belongs in your freezer at home to maintain its freshness. Items you find in an open or closed refrigerated section at the store should find similar spots in your refrigerator. For open display items, the fridge door or front shelves, which experience more temperature changes, are suitable. Items from a closed refrigerator should be stored toward the back of your fridge, where it's consistently cooler.

Pantry vs. Fridge for Produce: If your fruits and vegetables came from a dry bin, they're generally happy sitting in your pantry. However, if they were refrigerated at the store, they'll need to stay cool at home too. For those with climate-controlled crispers in their fridges, take note of the produce's storage at the store. Items kept under misters benefit from high humidity, while others prefer a cooler, dryer environment.

Become a 'Date Detective': Perishable goods like eggs, dairy, meats, poultry, and seafood often come with dates that hint at their freshness. But remember, these dates are more guidelines than strict rules, assuming proper storage on your part. That said, common sense is crucial; a piece of fish forgotten in a hot car overnight is a definite no-go, regardless of the date printed on the package. Familiarize yourself with terms such as "sell-by," "use-by", "best-by," "pack date," and "expiration date" to make informed decisions about your food's quality and safety.

Adopting these practices not only ensures that you enjoy your food to its best but also helps reduce waste by avoiding premature spoilage. Later in this chapter, we'll dive deeper into tips and tricks for extending the life of your perishables even further, helping you make the most of your groceries and your budget.

Perishables - Eggs: Cracking the Code

Diving into the world of eggs, you'll notice some terms on the carton that are quite helpful once decoded. The "pack date" simply tells you when the eggs were nestled into their carton homes. Then there's the "sell by" or "expiration" date, which is essentially the packer's educated estimate of when the eggs might start losing their fresh edge. But fear not, an egg's journey from prime to decline isn't a swift plunge - it's more of a gentle slide. Except, of course, in extreme conditions like a sweltering car trunk, where eggs can take a turn for the worse overnight.

Now, for the age-old question: How can you tell if an egg is still eager to be part of your next meal or if it's time to part ways? There's a neat little test for that. Place the egg in a bowl of water. Fresh eggs will stay at the bottom, while those past their prime will float. This happens because of an air bubble inside the egg that expands over time.

Before we crack on, here are two golden nuggets of advice to keep in your apron pocket: First, always inspect eggs at the store. Open the carton and look for any cracks. Think of a crack as an open door to bacteria - definitely not guests you want at your breakfast table. Second, even if an egg looks fine and is within its date, always crack it into a separate bowl before adding it to your recipe. This step is your safety net, ensuring one bad egg doesn't spoil the entire dish.

Remember, with eggs, as in cooking and life, a little bit of caution and a lot of knowledge go a long way.

Perishables - Meat, Chicken, Fish, and Dairy

Understanding dates on perishable items like meat, chicken, fish, and dairy is key to ensuring both quality and safety in your meals. The "pack date" tells you when the item was packaged, similar to eggs. Occasionally, you might see a "packed from frozen on date," indicating when an item was thawed and repackaged. This detail can help you gauge freshness, especially for items that don't stay fresh as long once thawed.

More critical, though, are the "best-by" and "use-by" dates. It's important to note these aren't "eat by" deadlines. Instead, think of the "best-by" or "use-by" date as a guideline for when the product is likely at its peak quality according to the experts who know it best. At home, consider this the "ideal to use by" timeframe. If an item still looks and smells like it should a little past this date, it's generally safe to consume. However, trust your senses - if anything seems off (in appearance, smell, or texture) before that date, it's wise to err on the side of caution and not use it.

Savvy shopping tip: Look out for discounted meats and dairy products nearing their "best-by" dates. Stores often reduce prices to move these items quickly, but that doesn't mean they're not worth buying. You can snag a great deal and either use it immediately, cook it, or freeze it for later use. Just make sure to do so on the day of purchase to maintain the quality and safety of the food. This approach not only saves money but also helps reduce food waste, aligning with a mindful and sustainable cooking practice.

Perishables - Fresh Produce Insights

Embracing fresh produce is a cornerstone of eating well. Engaging all your senses is key to choosing the best fruits and vegetables:

Vision: Feast your eyes on the colors. Bright, vivid hues often signal freshness, but also keep an eye out for any blemishes or bruises that could shorten shelf life.

Smell: Freshness has an aroma. Fruits and veggies should smell like the earth or their ripe selves, not musty or sour.

Touch: Get hands-on. Firmness (but not hardness) usually indicates something is ready to be enjoyed, whereas too much softness might suggest it's past its prime.

Hearing: Yes, listen! A melon that sounds hollow when you give it a gentle tap is usually juicier.

Taste: Although tasting isn't an option before you buy, remembering the flavors you enjoy will guide your selections. Look for textures and firmness that match your taste preferences to enhance your meals.

Fruits and Vegetables: From Robust Roots to Tender Greens

When you're at the grocery store, remember that fruits and veggies come with varying levels of resilience. Some are hardy travelers, while others are more delicate. Let's consider a 'produce durability spectrum':

Robust: These are your storage champions – potatoes, onions, and other root veggies. They're less fussy about conditions and can last longer.

Durable: A step more sensitive, this group includes items like broccoli and apples. They hold up well but appreciate a bit of extra care to stay fresh.

Delicate: Here we find the tender souls of the produce world, such as leafy greens and berries. They need immediate attention and care to keep them at their best.

Understanding these nuances ensures you'll not only select the freshest, tastiest produce but also manage your kitchen like a pro, minimizing waste and maximizing flavor.

Vegetable Wisdom

As you begin your grocery adventure, it's wise to arm yourself with a diverse array of vegetables for every occasion. Let's categorize them to simplify your shopping list and storage strategy.

Robust Vegetables: The Storage Warriors

Think of potatoes, onions, cabbage, Brussels sprouts, carrots, and other root vegetables like beets, turnips, and radishes as your kitchen allies. These hardy characters thrive in cool, dark places. Your local climate dictates their ideal home - sometimes the pantry, other times the fridge. Before you stash them away, remember: plastic bags are not their friends. These bags trap moisture, leading to unwanted mushiness. Instead, if your veggies come in plastic, add a paper towel to absorb excess moisture, ensuring a longer shelf life.

Keeping a trio of these robust vegetables on hand, with onions and potatoes as your go-to staples, ensures you're always ready to add depth and flavor to any dish. For an eco-friendly twist, both disposable and reusable paper towels work wonders for this moisture-wicking trick.

Durable Vegetables: Embrace Their Brief Beauty

Vegetables like broccoli and cauliflower have a fleeting freshness, reminding us to enjoy them while they're at their peak. They typically have a grace period of 2-3 days before they start to wilt and lose their vibrancy. To extend their prime time, you have options:

Give them the floral treatment: Place their stems in water to keep them perky and proud. This works well for asparagus and smaller broccoli heads, though larger cauliflower might require a different approach.

Prep and store: Peeling (where needed) and cutting into bite-sized pieces not only makes these veggies ready for action but also helps in preserving their freshness. After a quick wash (a pinch of baking soda can be your secret weapon here), pat them dry, and tuck them into a glass container with a paper towel layer below and above. This method is your best bet for extending the edible life of your produce and having ready-to-use veggies at your fingertips.

Delicate Vegetables: Handle with Care
Leafy greens and mushrooms might seem high maintenance, wilting at the slightest misstep. However, avoiding prepackaged options not only saves you money but also brings freshness to your meals. Spinach, kale, and lettuce, in their most unadulterated form, are not only economical but are vibrant additions to your meals. Washing, drying thoroughly, and storing them between paper towels can significantly extend their freshness, transforming them from perishable to perseverant.

By understanding these vegetable categories and their unique needs, you're not just shopping smarter; you're paving the way for a rainbow of nutritious, delicious meals that make the most of every ingredient.

Fruitful Savings: Mastering the Art of Smart and Sweet Choices
Navigating the fruit section as a savvy shopper can unlock a world of savings and flavor. Start by comparing the cost of whole fruits to their pre-cut counterparts. The price leap for convenience can be eye-opening. Embrace the empowerment of slicing your own fruits; it's not only economical but also a skill that serves you well. Upon returning home, give all your fruits a thorough wash. This prep step means you're always a quick reach away from a healthy snack.

Keeping fruits whole until you're ready to enjoy them preserves their freshness. Many fruits, especially those with edible skin, pack a nutritional punch right beneath their surface, so whenever possible, enjoy the peel for that extra fiber and nutrient boost. For fruits like grapes, keeping them on the stem can ward off premature browning at their bases. And if you're planning ahead for fruits prone to browning, such as apples, a little lemon juice can keep them looking appetizing and fresh.

Dessert Time

Fruits aren't just for snacking; they're also versatile culinary chameleons. An apple a bit past its prime? Transform it with a quick chop and a zap in the microwave. Sprinkle on some cinnamon, drizzle with honey, and voila - a delectable apple pie filling emerges. Elevate it to dessert status with a crunch of granola and a scoop of ice cream for an impromptu apple pie à la mode. The same can be done with peaches or bananas. This approach to fruits not only maximizes your grocery budget but also introduces an easy, creative twist to your eating routine, making each meal an opportunity for exploration and enjoyment.

Chapter 6

Safe Bites

Navigating the Path to a Secure Kitchen

The kitchen can be a hotspot for accidents and injuries, especially with sharp knives, hot stovetops, and the risk of fires or burns. However, by staying mindful and taking simple precautions, you can greatly reduce these risks and keep your cooking experience safe and enjoyable.

Food Safety Essentials

Ensuring the safety of the food you prepare is crucial to your well-being. Remember, it's not just about checking expiration dates and giving things a sniff test (though those are important too!). We trust that you're already using separate cutting boards for raw meats and produce, and that you're diligent about washing everything, including your hands, between uses. However, even with these precautions, the journey from the grocery store to your plate can still pose risks. But fear not! With a sprinkle of caution and a few key practices, your culinary escapades will keep you healthy and happy.

Fire Safety Tips

Stay Vigilant – Keeping an eye on your cooking is essential. Never leave the kitchen unattended, especially when using high heat. By staying attentive, you not only prevent potential disasters but also ensure your meal turns out perfectly without any unwanted surprises! While we don't expect you to stand guard over your oven for the entire cooking time, it's crucial to remain nearby. Set alarms on your phone to remind you to check on your food periodically. And here's a helpful tip: give each alarm a memorable name so you won't ignore it. Trust us, alarm fatigue is a real thing!

Fire Safety Alert – A smoke detector serves as your ultimate backup alarm in the event of a fire. If a fire occurs without your awareness, the smoke detector will sound, providing crucial warning to make a quick decision.

Staying Safe on the Cooktop – Whether you're using a cooktop, stovetop, or hot plate, safety should always come first. Remember to turn pot handles inward to prevent accidental spills, burns, or injuries. This simple practice reduces the risk of handles being bumped or grabbed unintentionally. And speaking of pot handles, they can get hot too! Keep oven mitts nearby while cooking to safely handle hot pots and pans.

With many stovetops featuring multiple burners, double-check that you're turning on the one you intend to use. Remember, burners can remain hot long after being turned off, so never assume they're cool – especially if you share living space with roommates.

When it comes to placing items on the cooktop, only use heat-proof materials. Even a split-second contact with a hot surface can lead to accidents. Treat the cooktop like it's a game of 'the floor is lava' – except with real heat!

Overflowing pots can be dramatic, but don't panic! If water spills onto a hot burner, lower the heat under the pot to quickly calm the situation. And if cooking gets a bit too intense – like your egg sizzling too hard or your stew bubbling like a geyser – remember these four steps: 1. Turn off the heat. 2. Don oven mitts. 3. Cover the pot with a lid. 4. Move pot from hot surface. Once things settle down, you can jump right back into your cooking adventure!

Oven Safety – Ovens are commonly positioned at floor level for easy access. It's important to be cautious when opening the oven door, as a rush of extremely hot air can escape. To prevent accidental burns, make sure to keep your face away from the opening to avoid singeing your eyebrows or getting burnt.

Ensuring Microwave Safety – Microwaves can be a convenient cooking tool, but they may heat food unevenly. It's important to be cautious to prevent burns. Always use oven mitts when handling dishes from the microwave, as they can become unexpectedly hot. To ensure your food is evenly heated, stir it thoroughly before eating or drinking to avoid encountering any overly hot spots that could burn your mouth.

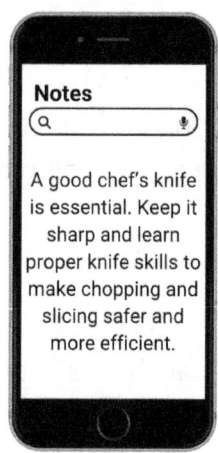

Notes

A good chef's knife is essential. Keep it sharp and learn proper knife skills to make chopping and slicing safer and more efficient.

If a Fire Occurs

Despite taking precautions, it's possible for a fire to break out in the kitchen. In such a situation, your safety is the top priority. Remember, things can be replaced, but your well-being cannot. Assess the situation calmly and determine if immediate action, such as calling 911, is necessary. Even if you initially feel in control, it's crucial to continually reassess the situation as fires can escalate rapidly.

If the fire is contained, such as in a pot or oven, the first step is to suffocate it. Remember, fire needs oxygen to thrive. For example, if flames appear in the oven, promptly turn it off and keep the door closed. This will help smother the fire, allowing it to gradually extinguish. Similarly, if a fire erupts in a pot on the stove, turn off the heat and cover it with a lid.

However, if the fire is not contained, such as on the stovetop, follow these steps:

1. Prioritize your safety above all else and ensure you have a clear path to exit the kitchen if needed.

2. Take precautions to protect yourself by wearing oven mitts, securing long hair, and rolling up loose sleeves.

3. Immediately turn off the source of heat or flame to prevent the fire from spreading further.

4. Remove any nearby flammable items, such as paper towels or kitchen towels, to prevent the fire from igniting additional hazards.

5. Evaluate the situation to determine if and how you can safely attempt to extinguish the fire. However, bear in mind that tackling a kitchen fire can be challenging and requires careful consideration, as we'll explore further in the following paragraph.

Fire Safety in the Kitchen: Protecting Yourself and Your Home

Understanding the seriousness of kitchen fires is crucial. It's essential to avoid using water to extinguish a kitchen fire, as it can worsen grease or electrical fires. Instead, having a fire extinguisher on hand is key. But here's the catch: you need to know how to use it before an emergency arises. Most extinguishers come with clear instructions – take the time to read them when you first get yours. Get familiar with your safety equipment to minimize surprises during an emergency. Store the extinguisher in a visible and easily accessible location, with the label facing outward for quick identification.

Practicing with a fire extinguisher is ideal, but the discharge is messy and only lasts a few seconds. It's also important to choose the right type of extinguisher for the fire at hand. There are two main types: Class K, specifically designed for grease fires, and multi-purpose ABC extinguishers for other types of fires. We've listed a convenient 2-pack under Resources to help you get started.

While fire extinguishers are vital, they can be intimidating. That's where a "fire blanket" comes in handy. Made of fire-resistant materials like fiberglass or wool, fire blankets work by smothering small fires, much like a very large lid. If you've ever made your bed (as you should every morning), you already know how to use a fire blanket.

Knife Safety: A Cut Above the Rest

Follow the golden rule: always opt for sharp blades in the kitchen. Contrary to intuition, dull knives pose a greater risk as they're more likely to slip, potentially leading to accidents. Keep your knives always honed and in prime condition. When wielding a knife, mindfulness is key - ensure your fingers and hands are safely distanced from the blade during cutting, slicing, or peeling tasks. A little caution can prevent a multitude of mishaps.

Additionally, maintain stability by working on a secure surface, and always direct your cutting motion away from your body. Not only does this practice guarantee safety, but it also raises precision in your culinary endeavors.

Once you've finished with your knives, store them securely - ideally in a sheath or knife block. This not only preserves their sharpness but also minimizes the risk of accidental cuts when reaching for them. Here's a helpful hint: refrain from tossing your knives in the dishwasher. The harsh environment can dull their edges and, depending on the detergent, may even cause rust or corrosion. Instead, opt for hand washing and thorough drying. Your knives - and fingers - will be ever grateful for the extra care.

Chapter 7

The Art of Time

Transforming Meals with Patience

Time is money. No expression rings truer than in a kitchen. It's no secret that convenience carries a price tag. Sometimes, it is wiser to pay a little extra to save time. What you'll want to avoid are last minute costly decisions brought on by a lack of preparation. You know what they say: fail to plan and you might as well plan to fail. Convenience is ubiquitous and attractive. Deliveries are contactless and don't even require talking to a person. You can order anything from the comfort of your couch. A clear head will weigh the cost benefit, but a "hangry" stomach screams louder than commonsense. Convenience has its place in the kitchen, as long as you control "it" and not the other way around. Realistically, you should aim for 80% carefully shopped, home-cooked, brown-bagged meals which should leave you with some extra money for splurge meals.

Surviving the Swipe: Why Food Apps Can Break the Bank

A simple push to a touch screen is all that separates your stomach from your favorite junk food. With a slew of delivery apps to choose from, a simple $2.85 burger easily turns into a $30 order. How? It's easy, add bacon to your burger ($1.10), some French fries ($2.15), and a large drink ($3.55). Now comes the fun part. Basic delivery fees add $4.99. You're hungry so you'll select "Express" service for only $2.99 more. Uncle Sam needs money too, so you'll pay almost $4 in taxes. Finally, the app will suggest a tip of $3.50 for your driver, who is probably a broke student like you, so you generously add $1.50 to the suggested tip. Just like that, you blew your entire weekly food budget just because you were hankering for a $3 burger.

Unless you can afford $30-burgers all day long, ordering in should be a treat, a reward for work well done. Maybe you decide to forego cooking for an afternoon of studying. If you follow the advice in this guide 80% of the time, you'll have money for a delivery splurge. Sometimes life will get in the way, and it will seem like the universe is conspiring against you: you are running late, the power goes out, and you forgot a term paper due tomorrow. That is when ordering in makes sense.

Meal Kits: Not Always the Best Recipe for Your Wallet or Creativity

While meal kits might seem like a convenient solution for busy college students, they often come with a hefty price tag and excessive packaging that can add up over time. While the idea of receiving pre-portioned ingredients and easy-to-follow recipes is appealing, the reality is that these services can be quite costly, especially on a tight budget. Additionally, the amount of packaging involved, from individual plastic-wrapped ingredients to insulated boxes and ice packs unnecessarily contributes to environmental waste.

On the other hand, meal kits can be a great option to try new recipes without having to gamble on ingredients that you may or may not like. Turn weekly meals into a roommate adventure! Explore cuisines with meal kits and split the prep work. Fun guaranteed!

Again, if you practice conscientious cooking most of the time, you should have funds available for a bit of controlled creativity and bridled spontaneity.

When Time is Money... and Taste

Good (tasting) things come to those who wait. The opposite of fast food could be described as "slow food." This term refers to food that is prepared with care, using traditional methods, often focusing on locally sourced and high-quality ingredients. Slow food emphasizes the importance of taking time to cook and enjoy meals, rather than opting for quick and convenient options like fast food or quick serve. Does that sound familiar? Is "slow food" the same as resourceful cooking? We think so.

Some cooking activities require your full attention, pan frying a fish for example doesn't allow for multi-tasking. However, many cooking basics require nothing but a little planning and the inexorable passage of time.

Sautéing – Every Great Chef's Simple Trick (20 minutes)

Onion, the inexpensive and mundane vegetable is also the invisible star of many elevated dishes. Delicious sauces, stews, and soups all start with a copious mount of onions sauteed for some time, 15 to 20 minutes. Onions are intimidating because they taste so strong when raw. Cook them long enough and they'll mellow out, become translucent and eventually melt into a delicious paste. Onions form the basis of many great cuisines. The French with their famously fancy cuisine have "Mirepoix", composed of ordinary onions, carrots, and celery. The Italians – no stranger to a delicious meal – call it soffritto. Many other cultures have their own versions of flavor bases similar to mirepoix, although they may contain different ingredients depending on regional culinary traditions. Three of the ten recipes in this guide (lentil soup, Bolognese sauce, and curry) start with onions. Trust the process, go heavy on the onions, and sauté for 15-20 minutes. This simple trick will raise your dishes from meal to experience.

Simmering – Take Your Time (30 minutes – 4 hours)

Simmering is a cooking technique where food is cooked gently in liquid at a temperature just below boiling. You'll typically encounter the instruction to simmer when cooking soups, stews, curries, or chillis. Simmering can take anywhere from 30 minutes to multiple hours. The wide range is maddening, although 30 minutes is the agreed minimum. Let's first go over "why" we must simmer, and then we'll cover "how" to simmer.

Simmering allows food to cook evenly and slowly while infusing flavor and tenderizing. This is particularly important for tougher cuts of meat as the gentle heat helps to break it down, resulting in tender and flavorful dishes. Stew meat should take 2-3 hours to break down. You may not have money for a porterhouse-type steak, but with a few hours on your hands you can prepare a meat that is tender and delicious. Use the blank pages at the end of this guide to note your ultimate cooking time and temperature. Create your own individualized cookbook based on your experience. "Your" recipe may read: use large green pot on rear left burner at "one line before low" for 1h45 minutes. By documenting your successes, you will soon go from "trial and error" to masterful cooking every time.

Vegetables don't take as long to soften. Our Hearty Lentil Soup recipe is a great example of a short simmer with great flavor. While lentils are small legumes that cook rapidly, larger dry beans may benefit from soaking – yet another "time is treasure" trick that we'll cover in this chapter.

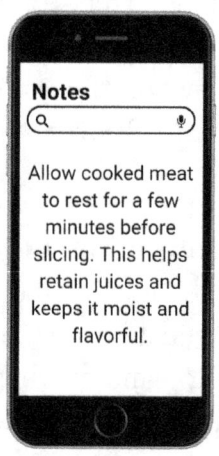

To cover or not cover: that is the question. Some recipes will instruct you to simmer covered, uncovered, or partially covered. That means the lid will cover the pot fully, not at all, or just a bit. Other recipes will instruct you to simmer without specifying a job for said lid. Here's how you decide. Simmering can help thicken your dish by reducing the liquid through evaporation. As the liquid simmers, water evaporates, leaving behind a thicker, more concentrated sauce or broth. For the water to evaporate, the lid must be off, so you simmer uncovered. If thickening is not desired, you may as well cover the pot since it will retain heat better, therefore cook faster.

Soaking (1 hour – overnight)

Soaking legumes such as large beans overnight in water helps to soften their texture and greatly reduce cooking time. Soaking legumes overnight (roughly 8-12 hours) can cut down cooking time by approximately 25% to 50%. If overnight is not an option, you can do a quick soak by boiling the beans for 2 minutes, turning off the heat, and letting rest for one hour.

Soaking grains can help to reduce their cooking time and improve their texture. Overnight oats are a popular breakfast dish made by soaking rolled oats in liquid overnight, typically in the refrigerator. The oats absorb the liquid and soften overnight, resulting in a creamy and ready-to-eat breakfast option in the morning.

Marinating – Soaking, but for Meats (30 min – 2 hours)

Chicken is an incredibly versatile and budget-friendly protein option. While it's a staple in many kitchens, the white breast meat can sometimes lack flavor and excitement. This is where marinating comes in handy. Marinating chicken not only boosts its flavor but also allows you to customize it to your personal taste preferences while keeping it moist and juicy. Think of marinades as the dressing for your chicken - they're composed of oil, acid, and flavor, just like salad dressings. Oil carries the flavors, while acid, like lemon juice, helps to tenderize the meat by breaking down muscle fibers. The best practice is to use enough marinade to cover about half of the meat, ensuring each piece gets infused with flavor. You can also place the chicken and marinade in a zippered bag and massage it for even distribution. If you're pressed for time, you can speed up the marinating process by poking the chicken with a fork to create channels for the marinade to penetrate faster. But be mindful of how long you marinate - the strength of your marinade determines the time needed. Lemon juice, for example, can start to "pre-cook" the meat if left too long. Remember, marinating doesn't fully cook the meat, so you'll still need to cook it thoroughly. If you're short on time, skip the marinating process altogether - less than 30 minutes won't make much of a difference.

The duration of your marination matters. The longer you marinate, the less intense your marinade needs to be. Save your more expensive ingredients, like a high-quality mustard, for occasions when you can marinate for at least 2 hours. This way, you can get away with using less and still achieve delicious results.

These marinating tips aren't just for chicken; they're versatile and can work wonders with pork as well, often referred to as the "other white meat." And don't forget, they're equally applicable to tofu, offering flavorful options for vegetarians and vegans alike!

You might have heard of brining, especially around Thanksgiving. Brining involves soaking meat in a saltwater solution to enhance juiciness and tenderness. But be cautious - too much salt can ruin the meat. Start with a small piece and document your process until you find the perfect balance. A bland piece of chicken can be saved with ketchup, but with experimentation, you'll discover the ideal salt-to-water ratio and duration for the ultimate flavor. Once you've cracked the code, jot it down in this guide for future reference.

While red meat typically doesn't benefit from marinating to the same extent as white meats like chicken or pork, it can still derive notable benefits from the process. Marinating red meat can indeed lift its flavor profile and tenderness, albeit to a lesser degree.

Don't marinate fish. Fish is delicate, and marinating it for too long or with acidic ingredients can cause its flesh to become mushy. Acidic ingredients like lemon juice or vinegar can "cook" fish, as seen in dishes like ceviche, where raw fish is marinated in citrus juices.

Resting (5 – 15 min)

Giving cooked meats a chance to rest is a crucial step often overlooked in the kitchen. Once your meat is done cooking, resist the temptation to dive right in. Instead, transfer it to a plate and let it rest. Worried about your meal getting cold? Simply cover the plate with aluminum foil or place an upside-down plate or bowl over the dish to keep the heat in.

Why is this resting period so important? Well, it allows the juices that have migrated to the surface of the meat during cooking to redistribute throughout, ensuring each bite is moist and flavorful. Plus, it gives the meat a chance to relax, resulting in a more tender and enjoyable texture. Slicing into meat immediately after cooking can cause those precious juices to escape, leaving you with dry and tough meat.

You don't need to wait long - just give your meat between 5 and 15 minutes to rest before digging in. It's worth the wait for that perfectly juicy and tender bite!

Reheating (5 – 45 min)

Cold pizza might seem like the ultimate breakfast of champions, but there are times when reheating leftovers can enrich your enjoyment. Before hastily popping a bowl in the microwave, take a moment to consider if a different - perhaps longer - reheating method could yield better results.

Dishes like soups and stews often taste even better the next day when reheated slowly. Here's a pro tip: instead of transferring leftovers to a separate container, simply cover the pot and place it in the refrigerator. This makes it super easy to reheat later on without creating extra dishes. It's not about being lazy; it's about thinking ahead and saving time.

Now, back to that pizza slice. Microwaving it might leave it disappointingly limp. But fear not! If you have a toaster oven or a pan handy, you can bring it back to life with a lovely crispy texture. Just use low heat and give it about 10-15 minutes - it'll be worth the wait for that perfect slice!

Chapter 8

Heat Masters

Tools that Turn Up the Temperature

Welcome to the heart of your kitchen adventure! Whether you're a seasoned cook or just starting out, mastering different heat sources is key to unlocking a world of possibilities. While a microwave is convenient, it's just one small piece of the cooking puzzle. Think of a microwave like a vending machine in a supermarket: great for a quick fix, but not for creating delicious meals. To truly master cooking, you'll need more versatile tools that offer different ways to apply heat to your food.

In this chapter, we'll introduce you to two essential sources of heat that will elevate your skills: direct and indirect heat. With these tools, you can whip up anything from a quick breakfast to a gourmet dinner. And the best part? You can get both for under $80.

Let's fire up those taste buds and see how these tools can turn your kitchen into a culinary playground!

A Word on Microwave

Living in dorms or other shared housing often means strict safety and fire regulations, which might limit your access to traditional heat-producing appliances. But fear not! A microwave can be a game-changer in your kitchen arsenal. With this versatile tool, you can cook pasta, steam vegetables, and even poach an egg. Microwaves are incredibly convenient for quickly heating water and leftovers, making them an essential appliance for many students.

If you have the space and budget, investing in a microwave is highly recommended. It's an excellent tool for a variety of quick and easy meals. However, while microwaves are fantastic for many tasks, they may not be the best choice for consistently cooking economical and nutritious meals on their own. Combining microwave use with other simple cooking methods will help you create a balanced and varied diet.

What's "Direct" Heat

Cooking with direct heat means placing food directly over or under the heat source. This method is perfect for boiling water, searing meats, grilling vegetables, or simmering stews.

If you have a cooktop or stovetop, you're working with direct heat! This is where the cooking elements are open and directly heat your pots and pans. It's great for tasks like boiling water for pasta, frying eggs, pan-frying chicken or fish, or sauteing vegetables.

No cooktop? No problem! A hotplate - a single electric element - can be a budget-friendly alternative. You can find one for around $20, making it a handy solution for tight spaces or temporary cooking setups.

Direct heat isn't limited to stovetops. Ovens also offer a direct heat option with their broil setting. When you set your oven to broil, the top heating element stays on, providing a steady, intense heat from above. This is ideal for quickly cooking food with a nice, crispy top, like melting cheese on a casserole or giving a golden finish to baked dishes. Broiling is similar to grilling but with the heat source above the food rather than below.

Understanding these basic cooking methods can help you master a variety of recipes and techniques, making your culinary adventures in college both fun and successful.

What's "Indirect" Heat

Indirect heat circulates around the food. Anything oven-baked, from cakes to roasts, uses indirect heat. Indirect heat is also great for reheating previously cooked meals because you can select a gentle low heat. You may be lucky and already have an oven as part of a range. Your oven is your portal to pastries, roasted meats and vegetables, or even dehydrating fruits for tasty snacks. You can also use your oven for slow-cooking tougher cuts of meat.

If you don't have a range, you can get an affordable toaster oven – a low-footprint versatile appliance perfect when cooking for one (or two). You can use a toaster oven to toast bread or bagels, reheat pizza, broil fish, roast vegetables, melt cheese, crisp tater tots, or bake a small cake. Toaster ovens also preheat faster than a full-size oven, making them energy efficient.

Even if you have the luxury of a range, you may wish to add a toaster oven to your tool arsenal for its versatility and ease in practicing "broiling". To broil in a toaster oven, set it to the broil function. Place the food on the broiler pan or a baking sheet, positioning it on the top rack of the oven, close to the heating element. You may want to keep the oven door slightly ajar to allow steam to escape and prevent overheating. Broiling is perfect for cooking foods that benefit from a quick, high-heat application, such as steaks, chicken breasts, pork chops, and fish fillets. They'll develop a flavorful crust while staying juicy inside. Root vegetables such as carrots, potatoes, and beets can be broiled to achieve a nice char and enriched flavor. Cheese-topped dishes such as casseroles, gratins, and open-faced sandwiches with melted cheese will get a deliciously crispy and golden topping on the broil setting. Are you hungry yet?

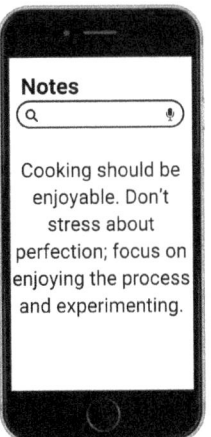

Many toaster ovens come with a built-in timer, which automatically shuts off the oven when the time is up. This feature helps prevent overcooking and adds a layer of safety. For instance, if you're baking a potato (one of our featured recipes), you might need to run the timer twice to achieve a perfectly baked spud.

Toaster oven's performances vary widely, so use the "Notes" section of this book to document your preferred times and temperatures. For example, a piece of fish can broil in as little as 8 minutes. Start with less time than you think you'll need, as you can always cook it a bit longer.

What About All Those Cool Gadgets?

You know the ones: they promise to save you time AND money, and a slew of new ones pops up every year with catchy names. Gadgets can be fun if you have the money to buy them, the space to store them, and the inclination to clean them. However, you can achieve the same results as a slow cooker or pressure cooker with a regular pot on the stovetop. And an air fryer? A rectangular toaster oven is far more versatile and can "air fry" as well.

Cast Iron Cookware – Treasured Heirloom

If you do decide to purchase a specialty item - or if Aunt Edna is determined to gift you one - consider a Dutch oven. This simple cooking pot is known for its thick walls and tight-fitting lid, and is usually made of cast iron, making it super heavy. Opt for an enameled one (coated with porcelain) to make cooking and cleaning a breeze. If you choose a traditional cast iron pan, remember that it requires seasoning, so do a bit of research on how to maintain it.

A Dutch oven is incredibly versatile. You can use it on the stovetop, in the oven, and even over an open flame, making it suitable for various cooking methods. You can use it for everything from baking bread to searing a steak and even deep-frying! Enameled Dutch ovens come in a variety of colors, making them not only practical but also beautiful enough to be displayed. Their durability makes them last for generations, so don't turn your nose up if Aunt Edna wants to give you her old one - that's an heirloom!

When choosing a Dutch oven, go for one that's between 5-7 quarts. This size is small enough for cooking for one or two, but large enough for meal planning.

There are three popular brands of Dutch ovens at different price points, all listed under our "Other Useful Items" resource list. Since your Dutch oven will last multiple lifetimes with proper care, this is one instance where a splurge is appropriate, especially if Aunt Edna is footing the bill.

Traditional Cast Iron Skillets

Cast iron skillets are a must-have for any kitchen. They are affordable, incredibly durable, and versatile, allowing you to cook over direct flame, in the oven, and on the stovetop. For convenience, look for pre-seasoned options. Consider getting a small skillet for eggs and pancakes, and a larger one for frying potatoes or meats. With proper care, these skillets will last a lifetime and become your go-to cookware for countless delicious meals. Cast iron provides even heat distribution, enhancing your cooking results, and can even add a small amount of iron to your diet. To maintain your skillet, clean it with hot water and a stiff brush, dry it thoroughly, and apply a thin layer of oil before storing to prevent rusting.

Simplifying Cleanup with Parchment Paper

Let's be real, scrubbing burnt-on cheese is not anyone's idea of a good time. That's where parchment paper comes to the rescue. By lining your toaster oven baking tray with parchment paper, you'll save yourself the hassle of dealing with baked-on messes. Parchment paper is available in rolls or pre-cut sheets. We prefer large sheets that can be cut to the desired size and don't curl up as much as rolls. Besides simplifying cleanup, parchment paper also prevents food from sticking to cooking surfaces. For an eco-friendly option, choose unbleached, compostable parchment paper.

Whichever heat source you choose, always pay attention and practice caution. Plan ahead, use timers, and double-check that everything is properly shut off before walking away. A little prevention can save you a lot of trouble and keep your kitchen safe.

Chapter 9

Effortless Eats

Simple Recipes for No-Stress Meals

Whether you're juggling classes, assignments, or simply craving a hassle-free bite, this guide is designed with you in mind. Discover how to whip up delicious dishes with minimal ingredients, time, and effort, all while keeping your budget intact. From quick on-the-go breakfasts to one-pot wonders and speedy snacks, you'll master the art of no-fuss cooking. Roll up your sleeves, put on your apron (or not), and dive into a world of simplicity and satisfaction.

We'll teach you 10 basic dishes and show you how to lift them into more impressive meals – over 50 of them! You'll also find tips for meal planning, grocery shopping, and making the most of leftovers. Get ready to build your confidence and enjoy the rewarding experience of cooking for yourself!

Chapter 10
Boiled Eggs

Guidelines to Make Boiled Eggs

Boiled eggs are a simple yet versatile cooking option that perfectly aligns with the practical needs and constraints of college life. Affordable, nutritious, and incredibly convenient, they are an essential addition to your repertoire. Whether you're looking for a quick breakfast, a protein-packed snack, or an ingredient to refine your meals, boiled eggs offer endless possibilities to suit your busy schedule and tight budget.

What You'll Need
-Pot with a lid
-Timer or smartphone
-Spoon
-Bowl (Tool #3)
-Covered container (Tool #5)

Ingredients
-As many eggs as you'd like (First grocery #1)
-Tap water
-Salt and pepper (Staples #3 and #4)
-Favorite condiment – optional (Staple #10)

Step-by-Step Instructions

Check for Freshness: Before you begin, it's good practice to use relatively fresh eggs. You can check their freshness by placing an egg in a glass of water; if it sinks and lays flat on the bottom, it's fresh. If it stands upright, it's not as fresh but still edible. If it floats, you'd better toss it than risk getting sick. In doubt, throw it out!

Prepare the Eggs: Place the eggs gently into a pot. You can cook as many or as few as you like, as long as they fit comfortably in a single layer.

Add Water: Cover the eggs with cold tap water. Make sure there's about an inch of water above the eggs. Add a pinch of salt to the water, which may make peeling the eggs easier later on.

Heat the Water: Place the pot on the stove over medium-high heat. Allow the water to come to a rolling boil.

Reduce Heat and Simmer: Once the water reaches a boil, reduce the heat to low and let the eggs simmer gently for about 9-12 minutes. Use a timer to ensure they don't overcook.

Adjust Boiling Time: To achieve your desired level of yolk doneness, you can experiment with the boiling time. For slightly softer yolks, reduce the boiling time by a minute or two; for firmer yolks, add a minute or two. Write down your preferred cooking time in the "Notes" section of this handbook.

Prepare an Ice Bath: While the eggs are simmering, fill your bowl with cold water (add ice cubes if available). This will be used to stop the cooking process and make the eggs easier to peel.

Drain and Cool: When the eggs are done, carefully use a spoon to transfer them to the ice bath. Let them sit for at least 5 minutes to cool down completely.

Peel and Enjoy: After cooling, tap each egg gently on a hard surface to crack the shell, then peel it off. Rinse any shell fragments away and pat the eggs dry. Peeling boiled eggs can sometimes be a bit tricky. Starting from the wider end where there's usually an air pocket often makes peeling easier.

Leveling Up

Sprinkle your boiled eggs with a pinch of salt and pepper for extra flavor.

Turn them into deviled eggs by slicing them in half, removing the yolks, mixing the yolks with your favorite condiment, salt, pepper, and then spooning the mixture back into the egg whites.

Using in a Greater Meal

Add boiled eggs to a fresh salad for added protein.

Serve them alongside toast or a simple sandwich for a classic breakfast.

Slice them and use as a topping with a bowl of noodles.

Storing Safely

Store your unpeeled boiled eggs in the refrigerator to keep them safe and fresh.

If peeled, keep them in a covered container to prevent any odors from affecting their taste.

Boiled eggs are versatile and can be enjoyed as a snack, added to various dishes, or turned into creative recipes. Learning how to boil eggs is a basic cooking skill that can open the door to a world of culinary possibilities, especially for college students living independently.

An egg can be a significant part of a meal and provide essential nutrients. Eggs boiled in their shell will last for a week in the refrigerator, providing you with an easy and mobile protein snack.

Chapter 11
4-Ingredient Salads

4-Ingredient Salads - 3 Easy Recipes

Salads are a fantastic way to enjoy a hearty meal filled with raw, healthy ingredients. Their vibrant colors make them visually appealing, but the delicate nature of greens like spinach or butter lettuce means they can wilt easily. Bagged salads, while convenient, can be twice the price of raw ingredients and have a shorter shelf life.

Making a salad can seem like a lot of work with all the washing and chopping, and their fragility often keeps them off the meal prep list. But we're about to change that. We're here to simplify the process, boost your nutrition intake, and lower your expenses with three easy 4-ingredient salads.

Put on some music, and let's get started!

What You'll Need
-Salad spinner (Tool #1)
-Cutting board (Tool #7)
-Knife (Tool #6)
-Vegetable peeler (Tool #10)
-Citrus juicer (Tool #2)
-Large bowl
-Paper towels
-Glass containers with lids (Tool #5)
-Baking soda (Staple #7)

Salad Kit – Easy Salad #1

Ingredients
-Kale
-Celery
-Red cabbage
-Carrots

Prepare the Kale

Kale is a hardy leafy vegetable that holds up to salad dressings for 24 hours. This makes it a great base for a meal-prep salad.

Add 2 tablespoons of baking soda to the salad spinner bowl. Grab each kale leaf by the stem and "peel" the leaves off. Discard the hard stems.

Place the kale leaves in the bowl and cover with cold water. Swish around with your hand for a few seconds to wash and dislodge impurities.

Grab handfuls of kale and place them in the salad spinner basket. Don't dump the kale and water into the basket, as this will also dump the dirt. By scooping the kale, you'll leave dirt and impurities in the bowl.

Place the lid on the salad spinner and spin the kale to remove excess water.

To chop the kale, grab a handful, form it into a tight ball, and slice thinly. Keep your fingers tucked away from the blade for safety. Take your time and maintain control of the blade.

Place the chopped kale in a large bowl.

Prepare the Celery

Cut off the bottom of the celery bunch. Inspect each stalk, removing any bruised parts.

Add 2 tablespoons of baking soda to the salad spinner bowl. Place the celery stalks in the bowl and cover with cold water. Rub each stalk clean.

Transfer the celery to the salad spinner basket to drip dry.

Thinly slice 4 whole stalks and add them to the large bowl with the kale.

To store the remaining stalks, place a dry paper towel on the bottom of a glass container with a lid. Add the celery, cover with another dry paper towel, and close the lid. Store in the refrigerator for up to 1 week.

Prepare the Red Cabbage

Slice off ¼ to ½ of the cabbage, depending on its size and your preference. Discard the outer blemished leaves.

Repeat steps 2 and 3 from the celery preparation instructions to clean and dry the cabbage.

Thinly slice the cabbage and add it to the large bowl.

To store the remaining cabbage, place a dry paper towel over the cut parts and store it in a large, zippered bag in the refrigerator for up to 2 weeks.

Prepare the Carrots

Wash and peel 4 carrots.

If you have a box grater, use it to grate the carrots. Otherwise, use your vegetable peeler to thinly slice them. Add the carrots to the large bowl.

Cut the remaining carrots into sticks for snacking. Store them like the celery and they will last over a week in the refrigerator.

Final Steps

Combine all prepared ingredients in the large bowl. This homemade salad kit will stay fresh for a week!

When ready to enjoy, portion some salad into a bowl, add your favorite dressing, and enjoy!

If your large bowl doesn't come with a lid, consider getting some silicone universal lids. This sturdy salad can be dressed hours in advance without wilting, making it perfect for lunch on the go.

Level it Up

Add a Protein: A can of tuna, a piece of chicken, some feta cheese, or a handful of nuts will turn this salad into a complete meal.

Extra Celery: Use your ready-to-go celery to level up an egg salad or to scoop hummus.

Extra Cabbage: When ready to use more cabbage, slice off and discard the exposed brown sides. Chop the rest, mix with olive oil, salt, and pepper, and roast on a parchment paper-covered tray for 20 minutes at 420 degrees Fahrenheit. Drizzle with balsamic vinegar and enjoy this healthy and colorful side dish.

Extra Carrots: Enjoy them on their own when you get a snack attack!

Greek Salad – Easy Salad #2

Ingredients:
-1 cucumber
-1 tomato
-½ lemon
-Greek seasoning

Prepare the Cucumber

Sprinkle a generous amount of baking soda on the cucumber.

Wet your hands and scrub the cucumber clean. The water will mix with the baking soda to form a lightly abrasive paste that will clean the cucumber effectively.

Rinse the cucumber thoroughly and let it drip dry in a salad spinner basket.

To reduce bitterness, cut off a small slice from the stem end of the cucumber and rub it in a circular motion against the cut end for about 10 seconds. Wipe away the white foam that forms.

Using a vegetable peeler, remove half of the cucumber's skin in alternating strips. Quarter the cucumber lengthwise and slice into ¼-inch pieces. If desired, remove the seeds before slicing.

Place the cucumber pieces in a large bowl.

Prepare the Tomato

Add 2 tablespoons of baking soda to the salad spinner bowl.

Place the tomato in the bowl, cover with cold water, and swish around.

Let the tomato drip dry in the salad spinner basket.

Depending on the type of tomatoes you have, you can leave them whole (for grape tomatoes), halve them (for cherry tomatoes), or cut them into bite-sized pieces.

Add the cut tomatoes to the bowl with the cucumbers.

Make the Dressing

In a small bowl, squeeze the juice of half a lemon.

Add 1-2 teaspoons of Greek seasoning, adjusting to your taste.

Whisk the lemon juice and seasoning together until well combined.

Final Steps

Pour the desired amount of dressing over the cucumber and tomato mixture.

Toss gently to coat all the ingredients evenly.

Store any unused dressing in a covered glass jar in the refrigerator.

Level it Up

Add black olives for extra flavor and a splash of color.

Add feta cheese for a protein boost and a creamy texture.

Summer Salad – Easy Salad #3

Ingredients:
-1 cucumber
-2 slices of watermelon
-Fresh mint leaves
-Tajín seasoning

Buying Watermelon

Buying a whole watermelon can be a big commitment due to its size and the space it takes up in your fridge. If you don't have enough space, consider buying a quarter watermelon.

A pre-cut quarter watermelon is slightly more expensive per pound than a whole one, but it's more economical than buying slices or pre-cut pieces.

Inspect the flesh of the quarter watermelon for freshness. Look for bright, deep red flesh with little to no white streaks. The flesh should appear fresh and juicy, not dry or discolored.

Buying Fresh Mint

Fresh mint is often sold in flat plastic packages or plastic cups with a vented dome. Choose mint leaves that are still on their stem.

To store, keep the stems in water like a bouquet of flowers and place in the fridge. Change the water daily to keep the mint fresh.

Prepare the Cucumber

Follow the instructions from the Greek Salad section to prepare the cucumber.

Place the cucumber slices in a large bowl.

Prepare the Watermelon

Cut a 2-inch slice from the watermelon quarter (or more if desired).

Remove any large black seeds.

Cut the watermelon into 1-inch pieces, discarding the rind.

Add the watermelon pieces to the large bowl with the cucumber.

Prepare the Mint

Pluck the mint leaves from the stems.

Rinse the leaves under running water and shake them dry.

Tear large mint leaves into smaller pieces and add them to the bowl.

Final Steps

Sprinkle a generous amount of Tajín seasoning over the salad.

Stir to combine, and add more Tajín to taste.

Level it Up

Grow Your Own Mint: If you enjoy mint, consider growing it yourself. Mint is an easy starter herb for budding gardeners.

Add Protein: For a heartier salad, add some crumbled feta cheese, grilled chicken, or chickpeas.

Chapter 12

Salad Dressing/Dip/Marinade

Guidelines to Make Dressings, Dips, or Marinades

This recipe is not just for salads; it's a versatile companion that can transform your meals from drab to delightful. Whether you're marinating proteins, dressing up veggies, or adding flavor to grains (First grocery #9), knowing how to create a simple dressing/marinade is a fundamental skill for college students. It's cost-effective, requires minimal tools, and allows you to customize your dishes with ease.

What You'll Need
-Large glass bowl (Tool #3)
-Citrus juicer or reamer (Tool #2)
-Knife (Tool #6)
-Cutting board (Tool #7)
-Glass food storage container (Tool #5)
-Whisk (or attachment of immersion blender) (Tool #9)

Ingredients
-Juice of 1 lemon (about 2-3 tablespoons) (Staple #1)
-Equal amount of olive oil (Staple #8)
-1-2 cloves garlic, minced (adjust to taste) (Staple #6)
-Salt and pepper to taste (Staples #3 and #4)
Optional: your favorite condiment (Staple #10) for heat, sweetness, or extra zing

Step-by-Step Instructions

Prepare Your Ingredients: Start by mincing the garlic cloves finely. You can use a knife and cutting board for this task.

Combine Olive Oil and Lemon Juice: In a large glass bowl, pour in the olive oil and squeeze the juice of one lemon over it. This combination forms the base of your dressing/marinade.

Add Minced Garlic: Toss in the minced garlic. Adjust the amount to your taste; one clove provides a mild garlic flavor, while two cloves offer a more robust kick. Add your condiment if you wish.

Season with Salt and Pepper: Season the mixture with a pinch of salt and a few cracks of black pepper. Remember, you can always add more later, so start with a small amount and taste as you go.

Whisk: Whisk until all the ingredients are well combined.

Taste and Adjust: Give your dressing/marinade a taste. If you'd like it tangier, add more lemon juice. Add salt, pepper, or your favorite condiment to taste.

Leveling Up

Herb Infusion: Lift your dressing/marinade with fresh or dried herbs like basil, oregano, or thyme.

Creative Variations: Experiment with different ingredients like balsamic vinegar, soy sauce, or grated Parmesan cheese for unique flavor profiles.

Using in a Greater Meal

Marinade: Use it to marinate chicken or tofu before grilling. Pour over a piece of fish just before broiling for added flavor.

Grain Bowl: Drizzle it over grain bowls to liven up your brown rice (First grocery #7) or quinoa.

Roasted Vegetables: Toss with veggies before roasting for a zesty side dish.

Storing Safely

Store any leftover dressing or unused marinade in a glass food storage container in the refrigerator.

It can be kept for up to a week. Shake or stir well before using leftovers.

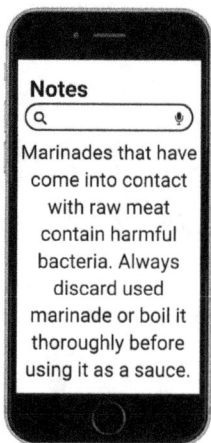

Notes

Marinades that have come into contact with raw meat contain harmful bacteria. Always discard used marinade or boil it thoroughly before using it as a sauce.

Fan-Favorite Daily Dressing

In a large bowl, squeeze the juice of half a lemon. Remove any seeds.

Add a splash of olive oil, 1 teaspoon of honey, 1 teaspoon of Dijon mustard, a shake of garlic powder, a shake of salt, and 6 turns of freshly ground black pepper.

Whisk the mixture for about a minute until it emulsifies.

Taste the dressing and adjust the seasoning as needed.

Chapter 13
Simple Tuna Salad Recipe

Guidelines for Turning Canned Proteins into Meals

Tuna salad is a lifesaver for busy college students. It's a quick, budget-friendly, and protein-packed recipe that can be whipped up in minutes. Whether you're craving a sandwich filling, a salad topper, or a snack with crackers, tuna salad has you covered. Plus, you can easily adapt this recipe using canned chicken for a tasty alternative.

What You'll Need
-Can opener (Tool #4)
-Knife (Tool #6)
-Cutting board (Tool #7)
-Large glass bowl (Tool #3)
-Glass food storage container (Tool #5)

Ingredients
-1 can of tuna or canned chicken, drained (First grocery #2)
-1/4 cup olive oil (or mayonnaise if you prefer) (Staples #8 or #10)
-1/4 cup diced celery (First grocery #3)
-2 tablespoons diced onion (First grocery #6)
-1 tablespoon lemon juice (Staple #1)
-Salt and pepper to taste (Staples #3 and #4)
Optional: Diced pickles, mustard, hard-boiled eggs, chopped ap-

ples, grapes, cranberries, or chopped nuts for added flavor and texture

Step-by-Step Instructions:

Prepare Your Ingredients: Start by draining the canned tuna or chicken and transfer it to a large glass bowl.

Add Binding Condiment: add ¼ cup of olive or any binding condiment of your choice such as mayo or mustard to the bowl with the tuna or chicken.

Dice Celery and Onion: Finely dice the celery and onion on your cutting board. Add them to the bowl with the other ingredients.

Lemon Juice: Squeeze 1 tablespoon of lemon juice over the mixture. This adds a refreshing zing to your salad.

Season with Salt and Pepper: Sprinkle a pinch of salt and a few cracks of black pepper into the bowl. You can always adjust the seasoning later, so start with a small amount.

Customize to Your Liking: Now comes the fun part! Customize your salad with optional ingredients like diced pickles for tanginess, mustard for extra flavor, hard-boiled eggs for richness, or chopped apples, grapes, cranberries, or nuts for added sweetness or crunch.

Mix and Taste: Use a fork or spoon to mix all the ingredients together thoroughly. Taste your tuna or chicken salad and adjust the seasoning as needed. You can also experiment with the texture, making it creamier or chunkier based on your preference.

Leveling Up

Herb Infusion: Upgrade your salad with fresh herbs like parsley or dill for a burst of freshness.

Nutty Crunch: Throw in some chopped nuts, like almonds or walnuts, for added texture and flavor.

Using in a Greater Meal

Tuna or Chicken Melt: Spoon your salad onto bread, top with cheese, and broil (toaster oven works best) until bubbly for a delicious melt.

Stuffed Avocado: Scoop your salad into halved avocados - a known superfood - for a healthy and satisfying meal.

Wrap it Up: Use your salad as a filling for wraps or pita pockets with veggies and a drizzle of dressing.

Storing Safely

Seal your salad tightly in a glass food storage container to maintain freshness.

Keep it refrigerated to prevent spoilage.

Chapter 14

Hearty Lentil Soup

Guidelines to Make Lentil Soup

Lentil soup is nutritious, budget-friendly, and a breeze to prepare. Whether you're looking for a comforting meal on a chilly evening or a hearty lunch to power through your day, lentil soup has got you covered. Plus, it's forgiving, allowing for variations based on what you have on hand.

What You'll Need
-Large pot or Dutch oven
-Knife (Tool #6)
-Cutting board (Tool #7)
-Large glass bowl (Tool #3)
-Salad spinner (Tool #1)
-Can opener (Tool #4)
-Glass food storage container (Tool #5)
-Immersion blender (Tool #9)
-Vegetable peeler (Tool #10)
-Pyrex measuring cup (Tool #8)

Ingredients
-1 cup dried green or brown lentils (First grocery #5)
-1 onion, diced (First grocery #6)
-2 carrots, peeled and diced (First grocery #3)
-2 celery stalks, diced (First grocery #3)
-2 cloves garlic, minced (Staple #6)
-1 can (14 ounces) diced tomatoes (First grocery #4)

-6 cups vegetable or chicken broth (Staple #2)
-2 tablespoons olive oil (Staple #8)
-1 teaspoon cumin (optional)
-Salt and pepper to taste (Staples #3 and #4)
Optional: Fresh spinach, kale, bell peppers, or spices like paprika, turmeric, or red pepper flakes for customization

Step-by-Step Instructions

Rinse and Drain Lentils: Start by rinsing the lentils under cold water in your salad spinner bowl. Drain using the salad spinner basket and set them aside.

Sauté Aromatics: In a large pot, heat 2 tablespoons of olive oil over medium heat. Add diced onions, carrots, and celery. Sauté until they start to soften, about 5 minutes.

Add Garlic and Spices: Stir in minced garlic and cumin (if using) and cook for an additional minute until fragrant. You can also experiment with other spices like paprika, turmeric, or red pepper flakes for added depth.

Combine Lentils and Broth: Add the drained lentils, canned diced tomatoes (don't drain), and 6 cups of vegetable or chicken broth to the pot. Stir everything together. If you have fresh spinach, kale, or bell peppers, now is the time to add them for extra nutrients and flavor.

Simmer: Bring the mixture to a gentle boil, then reduce the heat to low and let it simmer for about 20-25 minutes, or until the lentils are tender.

Blend for Creaminess: For a creamier texture, take out about 1 cup of the soup using a ladle and blend it with an immersion blender until smooth. Then, return the blended mixture to the pot and stir well. You can choose how much to blend to suit your preference, from lightly creamy to completely smooth.

Season to Taste: Season your soup with salt and pepper to taste. Remember, you can always add more later, so start with a little. Feel free to adjust with your preferred spices too.

Leveling Up

Gourmet Garnishes: Top your soup with a dollop of Greek yogurt, a sprinkle of fresh herbs like parsley or cilantro, or a few slices of creamy avocado.

Using in a Greater Meal

Soup and Sandwich: Pair your lentil soup with a grilled cheese sandwich or a hearty salad for a well-rounded meal.

Lentil Stew: Thicken it up by adding more lentils, vegetables, and broth, turning it into a hearty stew. You may even add cooked sausages!

Storing Safely

Cooling: Let cool to room temperature before storing.

Refrigerating: Transfer the soup to an airtight container and refrigerate within 3 hours of cooking. It will last for up to 4 days.

Freezing: For longer storage, place the soup in freezer-safe containers or bags. It can be frozen for up to 3 months. To thaw, leave it in the refrigerator overnight or use the defrost setting on your microwave.

Reheating: Reheat on the stove over low heat, stirring occasionally, until heated through. You can also reheat in the microwave, stirring every minute until hot.

Chapter 15
Baked Potato

Guidelines to Make a Baked Potato

A baked potato (First grocery #9) is a perfect meal for college students learning to cook. It's super easy to make with just a potato, some oil, and a toaster oven. Potatoes are inexpensive, nutritious, and versatile, offering a great base for a variety of toppings like cheese, veggies, or lean meats. Plus, you can use leftovers in salads, soups, or breakfast dishes. They're a comforting, satisfying option that fits various diets, whether you're vegetarian, vegan, or gluten-free. Overall, baked potatoes are a simple, affordable, and tasty way to get a healthy meal without much fuss.

What You'll Need
-Toaster oven
-Small baking tray – one usually comes with the toaster oven
-Fork
-Parchment paper

Ingredients
-1 or 2 large russet potato (First grocery #9). Russet potatoes are best for baking due to their starchy texture.
-Olive oil (Staple #8)
-Salt (Staple #4)

Step-by-Step Instructions

Clean the Potato: Wash the potato thoroughly under running water. Use a brush to scrub off any dirt.

Dry the Potato: Pat the potato dry with a clean towel or a paper towel.

Preheat the Toaster Oven: Set your toaster oven to 400°F (200°C) and let it preheat.

Pierce the Potato: Use a fork to poke several holes around the potato. This helps steam escape during cooking.

Season the Potato: Drizzle olive oil over the potato and rub it evenly across the surface. Sprinkle salt over the potato, ensuring even coverage.

Bake the Potato: Place the potato directly on the baking tray or on a piece of parchment paper on the tray. Put the tray in the preheated toaster oven. Bake for 45-60 minutes, depending on the size of the potato. It's done when a fork easily pierces through the skin and flesh.

Check for Doneness: Carefully remove the potato from the toaster oven using oven mitts. Check if it's done by piercing it with a fork; it should be tender all the way through.

Serve: Let the potato cool for a few minutes. Cut it open and fluff the inside with a fork.

Leveling Up

Cheesy Delight: Top with shredded cheese and return to the toaster oven for a few minutes until the cheese melts.

Loaded Potato: Add sour cream, chopped green onions, crispy bacon bits, and a sprinkle of chives.

Healthy Twist: Add a dollop of Greek yogurt, steamed broccoli, and a sprinkle of nutritional yeast.

Southwest Style: Top with black beans (First grocery #8), corn, salsa, and a squeeze of lime.

Using in a Greater Meal

Potato Skins: Scoop out the flesh, mix it with cheese and bacon bits, fill the skins, and bake until crispy.

Potato Salad: Dice the baked potato, mix with mayonnaise, mustard, chopped pickles, and celery for a hearty potato salad.

Soup Thickener: Mash the potato and add it to soups for added creaminess and texture.

Breakfast Hash: Cube the baked potato and sauté it with onions, bell peppers, and your favorite breakfast sausage.

Storing Safely

Cool Down: Let the potato cool completely at room temperature.

Refrigerate: Store in an airtight container or wrap in aluminum foil. Keep in the refrigerator for up to 3-4 days.

Reheat: Reheat in the toaster oven at 350°F (175°C) for 10-15 minutes, or until warmed through.

Chapter 16
Bolognese Sauce

Guidelines to Make a Tomato Sauce with Meat

Bolognese sauce is an excellent meal choice because it combines simplicity with depth of flavor, making it both accessible and impressive. The ingredients are affordable and easy to find, and the recipe's step-by-step process teaches essential cooking techniques like browning meat, simmering, and seasoning. Bolognese is also highly versatile, allowing you to create a variety of dishes from one base sauce, such as pasta, lasagna, Frito pie, chili, or even a hearty pizza topping. Moreover, it can be made in large batches, making it perfect for meal prepping and ensuring that you have delicious, home-cooked meals ready throughout the week. The rich, comforting flavors of Bolognese not only satisfy but also provide a sense of accomplishment, boosting culinary confidence in an easy, approachable way.

What You'll Need
-Large pot with a lid – a Dutch oven is ideal
-Can opener (Tool #4)
-Knife (Tool #6)
-Cutting board (Tool #7)
-Large cooking spoon to stir
-Vegetable peeler (Tool #10)

Ingredients
-2 tbsp olive oil (Staple #8)
-3 onions, finely chopped (First grocery #6)

-2 carrots, peeled and finely chopped (First grocery #3)
-2 celery stalks, finely chopped (First grocery #3)
-2 garlic cloves, minced (Staple #6)
-2 lb. of ground beef or ground bison
-1 cup of broth (Staple #2)
-1 large (28 oz) can of diced tomatoes (First grocery #4)
-2 tbsp tomato paste*
-Salt and pepper to taste (Staples #3 and #4)
Optional: Fresh basil or parsley for garnish
Optional: Grated Parmesan cheese for serving
* Buy tomato paste in a tube if available. If you buy the small 6 oz can, use half and freeze the other half.

Step-by-Step Instructions

Prep the Vegetables: Wash, peel, and finely chop the onion, carrots, and celery. Mince the garlic.

Cook the Vegetables: Heat the olive oil in a large pot over medium heat. Add the chopped onion, carrots, and celery. Cook, stirring occasionally, for about 15 minutes until the vegetables are soft and the onion is translucent. Add the minced garlic and cook for another 5 minutes.

Brown the Meat: Increase the heat to medium-high and add the ground meat. Break it up with a wooden spoon and cook until browned all over. This should take about 8-10 minutes.

Add Broth: Pour in the broth and stir to combine. Let it simmer until the broth has mostly evaporated, about 10 minutes. This step adds richness and tenderness to the meat.

Add Tomatoes: Stir in the canned tomatoes and tomato paste. Reduce the heat to low and let the sauce simmer gently, uncovered, for at least 1.5 to 2 hours. Stir occasionally and add broth if the sauce starts to dry out.

Season: Season the sauce with salt and pepper to taste. Taste and adjust the seasoning as needed.

Serve: Serve the Bolognese sauce over your favorite pasta. Garnish with fresh basil or parsley and a generous sprinkle of grated Parmesan cheese if desired.

Leveling Up

Add Bacon: Add cooked bacon pieces before adding the tomatoes for extra flavor.

Use Different Meats: Try a mix of ground beef, pork, bison, and veal for a more complex flavor. You can also use meat alternatives or crumbled tofu.

Add Vegetables: Finely chop broccoli or cauliflower and add them along with the vegetables.

Improve with Herbs: Add a bay leaf or a sprig of thyme to the sauce as it simmers.

Boost with Umami: Add a splash of Worcestershire sauce or a bit of soy sauce for an umami kick.

Use stew meat: Instead of ground beef and you have a stew!

Add beans (First grocery #8): Add a can of beans to make chili. Or don't add beans and call that chili!

Using in a Greater Meal

Jacket Potato: ladle your sauce over a baked potato as an alternative to pasta.

Frito pie: open a bag of Fritos and add Bolognese. Top with cheese, raw onions, or whatever tickles your fancy.

Use rice (First grocery #7): Instead of pasta for a fun twist.

Lasagna: Layer the lasagna noodles with Bolognese sauce, béchamel sauce, and cheese for a classic lasagna.

Stuffed Peppers: Mix Bolognese with cooked rice (First grocery #7), stuff into bell peppers, and bake until the peppers are tender.

Shepherd's Pie: Use Bolognese as the base, topped with mashed potatoes (First grocery #9) and baked until golden.

Sloppy Joes: Serve the Bolognese on toasted buns for a twist on sloppy joes.

Pizza Topping: Spread Bolognese sauce on pizza dough, top with mozzarella, and bake.

Storing Safely

Cooling: Let the Bolognese sauce cool to room temperature before storing.

Refrigerating: Transfer the sauce to an airtight container and refrigerate within 2 hours of cooking. It will last for up to 4 days.

Freezing: For longer storage, place the sauce in freezer-safe containers or bags. It can be frozen for up to 3 months. To thaw, leave it in the refrigerator overnight or use the defrost setting on your microwave.

Reheating: Reheat on the stove over low heat, stirring occasionally, until heated through. You can also reheat in the microwave, stirring every minute until hot.

Additional Tips

Cooking Time: The longer you simmer the sauce, the better the flavor. If you have the time, let it go for 3-4 hours.

Consistency: If the sauce is too thick, add a bit of broth. If it's too thin, let it simmer uncovered until it reaches the desired consistency.

Pasta Water: When cooking pasta, save a cup of the pasta water. Adding a splash of this starchy water to the Bolognese sauce can help it adhere better to the pasta.

Portioning: Consider portioning out the sauce before freezing so you can defrost only what you need for a single meal. The "Souper cube freezing trays" listed under "Other Useful Items" are perfect for that purpose.

Chapter 17
Baked Chicken Breast

Guidelines to Bake a Chicken Breast

Knowing how to prepare a chicken breast is a valuable skill for any new cook, especially for college students starting to navigate their own kitchens. Chicken is the most consumed type of meat in the USA, with the average American eating nearly 100 pounds annually. This popularity is due to several factors: chicken is an affordable, lean source of protein, especially the white meat, which supports a healthy diet. Additionally, chicken breasts are versatile and can be easily incorporated into a variety of dishes, from salads to sandwiches to main courses.

Chicken cooked in a toaster oven can sometimes look unappealing without the char marks from a grill. To add a vibrant and appetizing color, sprinkle paprika or chili powder over the chicken prior to baking.

What You'll Need
-Citrus juicer (Tool #2)
-Glass container (Tool #5)
-Immersion blender (Tool #9)
-Fork
-Knife (Tool #6)
-Cutting board (Tool #7)
-Meat mallet – you can use a small cast iron skillet
-Zippered bag
-Parchment paper

-Paper towel
-Small strainer
-Toaster oven

Ingredients
-1 chicken breast
-1 lemon, juiced and strained to remove seeds and pulp
-Olive oil
-Garlic
-Greek seasoning
-Italian seasoning
-Pepper
-Paprika or chili powder for color

Step-by-Step Instructions

1. Trim the Fat

Remove Excess Fat: Trim off any visible fat from the chicken breast using a sharp knife.

Pat Dry: Pat the chicken breast dry with a paper towel to ensure better browning.

Tenderize: Place the breast on a cutting board and pierce it about 10 times with a fork. This helps the marinade penetrate the meat.

2. Pound the Chicken

Cover It Up: Wrap the chicken in a kitchen cloth or multiple paper towels. This prevents mess and helps protect the chicken from tearing. If using a kitchen cloth, put it in the laundry hamper immediately following use.

Pound Evenly: Using a meat mallet or a cast iron pan, gently pound the chicken to an even thickness, starting from the center and moving outwards. This ensures the chicken cooks evenly.

3. Marinate the Chicken

Prepare the Marinade: In a glass container, mix the following ingredients:
-Lemon juice
-3 tablespoons of olive oil
-1 clove of garlic, minced
-1 teaspoon of Greek seasoning
-1 teaspoon of Italian seasoning
-6 turns of freshly ground black pepper

Blend: Use an immersion blender to blend the ingredients into a creamy sauce.

Marinate: Pour the marinade into the resealable bag with the chicken. Remove as much air as possible, seal the bag, and place it on a plate in the refrigerator to catch any leaks. Marinate for 2-3 hours, flipping the bag occasionally to ensure even coverage.

4. Cook the Chicken

Preheat the Toaster Oven: Set your toaster oven to 375°F (190°C).

Prepare for Baking: Remove the chicken from the marinade, tap dry with a paper towel, cover with paprika or chili powder to give it a nice healthy color, and place on a baking tray lined with parchment paper.

Bake: Bake the chicken in the preheated toaster oven for 20 minutes, or until the internal temperature reaches 165°F (74°C). Cook longer if necessary, adding 5 minutes at a time.

Check for Doneness: Use a Thermometer: Use a meat thermometer to ensure the chicken has reached an internal temperature of 165°F. If you don't have a thermometer, cut into the thickest part of the chicken to check that the juices run clear and there is no pink meat.

Rest: Place the cooked chicken on a plate. Cover the plate with aluminum foil for 5 minutes, allowing the chicken to rest before slicing to let the juices redistribute.

Clean Up

Sanitize: Thoroughly clean any surfaces, utensils, and cutting boards that came into contact with the raw chicken using hot, soapy water. Raw chicken can contain salmonella, so it's important to ensure everything is properly sanitized.

Serve with Elegant Sides

Roasted Vegetables: Serve the chicken with a side of roasted vegetables like carrots, asparagus, or Brussels sprouts.

Grain Salad: Pair it with a refreshing grain salad made from quinoa, couscous, or farro, mixed with fresh herbs, cherry tomatoes, and a light vinaigrette.

Chapter 18

Elevate Your Cooking Game

Beyond the Basics

You've mastered the basics, and now it's time to dive into the fun and rewarding side of cooking that goes beyond just getting by. This chapter is about embracing the joy of creating something special - whether it's brewing the perfect cup of coffee at home, crafting a dish to impress friends, or simply finding delight in the process of cooking. Let's explore new techniques, flavors, and recipes that will make your time in the kitchen enjoyable and satisfying.

Have you ever heard the story of the Caesar salad? Legend has it that it was created by accident in Tijuana, Mexico, by Caesar Cardini, an Italian immigrant and restaurateur. One busy Fourth of July weekend in 1924, Caesar Cardini improvised a salad with the ingredients he had on hand, and it turned out to be a culinary masterpiece that we enjoy to this day. Just like Caesar's serendipitous creation, "Intro to Food" can be an artful blend of creativity and practicality.

Imagine the satisfaction of starting your day with a homemade latte, crafted exactly to your taste, or the pride of presenting a beautiful meal to a date, knowing that you've put your heart into every detail. "Intro to Food" is more than just a guide to feeding yourself - it's about creating memorable experiences and enjoying the process of cooking. Let's dive into tips, tricks, and recipes that will not only enhance your kitchen skills but also bring you joy.

Pick Your Fuel: Coffee, Tea, or Soda

Odds are, you rely on one of these delicious beverages to get you through the day. If you don't: bravo! For the rest of us, our daily drink is a comforting habit that helps us stay energized. However, having these beverages on the go can be costly and generate a lot of single-use waste. Here's how to enjoy your favorite drinks more sustainably and economically:

Coffee Break

If you're a regular coffee drinker, consider investing in a coffee maker and a reusable mug. You can find a simple drip coffee maker for less than $30, roughly the price of five specialty drinks at Starbucks. Spend a few extra dollars at the supermarket for sweeteners, caramel, and whipped cream, and you can become your own barista!

If you prefer single-serve coffee makers, a small Nespresso machine might be a good choice. They start around $140, and each pod costs about a dollar. Plus, they come in a variety of flavors to suit your tastes.

Teatime

For tea lovers, a kettle - either electric or stovetop - is a great investment. However, if you're looking for a more versatile option, a Pyrex measuring cup and a microwave can heat your water just as well. Pair this with an insulated mug of your choice, and you can enjoy hot tea all day long.

Soda/Pop/Soft Drink/Coke

Whatever you call it, soda has a strong appeal. If you're trying to limit your consumption, there are many economical and tasty alternatives. Water additives come in tablets, powders, or drops, and some even contain caffeine, electrolytes, or vitamins. You can mix them with plain water or unsweetened seltzer for a refreshing, fizzy treat.

By making small changes and smart purchases, you can enjoy your favorite beverages without breaking the bank or generating unnecessary waste.

Frozen Staples

A well-stocked freezer can be a game-changer for anyone starting to cook for themselves. Freezing opens a wide array of food options, from storing pre-made meals and frozen produce to keeping meats and dairy products fresh for longer. With a bit of planning, you can reduce food waste and always have ingredients on hand for quick, nutritious meals.

Frozen Vegetables

Frozen vegetables are a fantastic addition to your kitchen. They retain most of their nutrients, even though the freezing process may change their texture. Experiment to find what you like best. The simplest way to prepare frozen vegetables is to steam them in the microwave. Place a portion of vegetables in a glass bowl with a vented lid, add enough water to cover the bottom, and microwave for 2 minutes. Add more time if needed, and taste to check if you like the texture. If you do, drain the water and add the vegetables to cooked rice, serve them over pasta, or mix with chicken for a quick dinner. If the texture isn't to your liking, blend the vegetables with two cups of prepared broth to make a delicious cream soup. Season to taste.

Frozen Fruits
Frozen fruits are another convenient option, retaining most of their nutrients while losing some texture. They are perfect for desserts. Place a portion of frozen fruit in a bowl and microwave for one minute. The fruit will soften and release delicious juices. Add a sweetener like honey or maple syrup if you prefer, then top with plain yogurt or ice cream and garnish with granola for a quick and tasty treat. This method works best with berries. If you find the texture of thawed fruits unappealing, use an immersion blender to turn them into nutritious smoothies. You can add your favorite milk and even protein powder. For an extra boost, throw in a small amount of frozen kale or spinach for essential nutrients without changing the taste.

Tablescape

Sometimes, scarfing down a hastily prepared sandwich while hunched over the sink is all you have time and energy for. That should be the exception, not the rule.

Try to dedicate time not only to preparing your food but also to enjoying it. For a few dollars, you can elevate your dining experience with placemats, cloth napkins, and napkin rings. Washable placemats and napkins in neutral colors are practical choices, and seasonal napkin rings can add a touch of festivity. If you're worried about stains, opt for dark-colored items where stains won't show. Drinking a beverage from a glass rather than straight from the can makes it taste a million times better. Setting a table for yourself, especially away from your laptop, can transform your meal into a moment of relaxation and enjoyment.

Take a deep breath, engage your senses, and take a moment for gratitude. Investing a little time and effort into your tablescape will make your meals more satisfying and memorable.

Spice Mixes

Navigating the spice aisle at the supermarket can be overwhelming, and those small jars can add up quickly. To save both time and money, consider using spice mixes such as Italian herbs, taco seasoning, Greek seasoning, Sazón, Tajin, and Old Bay. These pre-mixed blends can simplify your cooking process and add a burst of flavor to your dishes.

Don't be afraid to get creative with these spice mixes. For example, try using taco seasoning to give your Bolognese sauce a unique twist. Old Bay, typically used for seafood, can also add a delicious kick to baked potatoes. When following a recipe, you'll often see a long list of individual herbs and spices. In many cases, you can replace these with a few shakes of a premixed blend.

A word of caution: most spice mixes already contain salt and pepper, so be sure to taste your dish before adding any extra. Here are some quick substitution tips:
If a recipe calls for basil, oregano, thyme, rosemary, or marjoram, use *Italian seasoning*.
If a recipe calls for garlic or onion powder, use *Greek seasoning*.
If a recipe calls for paprika, celery salt, bay leaves, or allspice, use *Old Bay*.
If a recipe calls for coriander or cumin (with a little kick), use *Sazón*.

To add some vibrancy to beige foods like egg whites, tofu, or baked chicken breasts, use paprika or chili powder for a burst of color and an extra layer of flavor.

Feel free to mix different premixes together to create your own unique flavor profile.

Experimenting with spice blends is a great way to discover what you like and make your meals more enjoyable. "Intro to Food" is about making the most of what you have, finding great deals, and being a savvy shopper. With these tips in mind, you'll be well on your way to creating delicious and budget-friendly meals as an independent adult. And who knows, you might even stumble upon your own culinary masterpiece, just like Caesar Cardini did with his famous salad.

Chapter 19

Beyond the Basics - Shrimp Dish

Guidelines for a Simple Shrimp Dish for Two

It's time to roll up your sleeves and put all your newfound knowledge to the test with a dish that is deceptively simple yet extraordinarily delicious. This recipe combines shrimp, tomatoes, and feta cheese to produce an exhilarating mix of flavors and a beautiful plate sure to impress.

Buying Shrimp
Shrimp is a wonderful protein that is naturally mild in flavor and forgiving to cook while feeling fancy. That makes them the perfect main ingredient for a refined dish that's as easy to prepare for one as it is to craft for a dinner date. You can buy fresh shrimp in the seafood section of any supermarket if you're ambitious enough to peel and devein them. Buying ready-to-cook frozen shrimp is a small splurge that will greatly ease the preparation of this dish. We recommend large shrimp – jumbo shrimp is expensive and medium shrimp don't present as well – large are just perfect. Read the packaging carefully. You want peeled, deveined, tail-off, raw, large shrimp. A 2-lb bag will contain between 40 and 50 shrimp, enough for 4 or 6 meals.

Choosing Tomatoes
Select small tomatoes, either cherry or grape tomatoes. They hold their shape better than their larger counterparts and are much easier to portion.

Feta Options

If you prioritize flavor, texture, versatility, and economy, go for block feta. It might take a little extra time to crumble it yourself, but the difference in quality is usually worth it. Block feta is usually half the price of its crumbled counterpart. If convenience is your main concern and you're in a rush, pre-crumbled feta can be a handy option.

What You'll Need
-Salad spinner (Tool #1)
-Knife (Tool #6)
-Cutting board (Tool #7)
-Large bowl (Tool #3)
-Whisk (Tool #9)
-Sheet-pan or oven tray (a toaster oven with a tray is ideal)

Ingredients
-2 tbsp olive oil (Staple #8)
-1 garlic clove, minced (Staple #6)
-1 lemon (Staple #1)
-Pepper (Staple #3)
-½ teaspoon salt (Staple #4)
-1 teaspoon Italian herbs (preferred, but optional)
-½ teaspoon of Sazon or Old Bay
-20 shrimp (calculate 8-12 shrimp per person)
-1 pack of cherry or grape tomatoes (10 oz)
-2-3 oz feta crumbled

Step-by-Step Instructions

Prep the Tomatoes: Place tomatoes in a salad spinner bowl with a tablespoon of baking soda. Swirl with your hand to wash. Transfer to the salad spinner basket to drain. Dry the salad spinner bowl. Halve or quarter the tomatoes and place them in the salad spinner bowl.

Prep the Feta: Slice 2 ounces of feta off the block. Chop coarsely to resemble large crumbles. Add to the salad spinner bowl with the tomatoes. Mix the tomato and feta.

Prep the Lemon: Slice a lemon in half. Juice one half, and quarter the other half to serve as a garnish. Remove all visible seeds from the quartered pieces. Pour lemon juice in large bowl.

Thaw the Shrimp: Place 20 frozen shrimp in the salad spinner basket. Run cold water over the shrimp until thawed, about 2 minutes. Let them drip dry.

Prepare the Sauce: In a large bowl using a whisk, mix the minced garlic, salt, Italian seasoning, lemon juice, olive oil, black pepper (a generous amount), and Sazón or Old Bay. The sauce should be thick and well-emulsified.

Season the Shrimp: Add the thawed shrimp to the sauce. Mix well, using your hands if you wish. Make sure each shrimp is thoroughly coated.

Preheat the Toaster Oven: Turn on the broiler and position the rack high up close to the heat.

Cook the Shrimp: Place a sheet of parchment paper on the oven tray. Make sure the parchment paper covers the tray but doesn't stick up to touch the red-hot cooking element. Spread the shrimp on the tray in one layer. Broil on one side for 3 minutes. Flip the shrimp and broil on the other side for 3 minutes.

Check the Shrimp: After 6 minutes, the shrimp should be perfectly cooked. To verify, cut into a shrimp. It should be slightly firm and not mushy. The flesh should be opaque all the way through with no translucent or grayish parts. Don't overcook the shrimp or they'll get rubbery.

Serving Tips

Divide the shrimp onto two plates and cover with the tomato/feta mix. Crack some black pepper on top. Wipe sauce splatter off the rim of each plate. Place two pieces of lemon on each plate for squeezing.

Set the table with a tablecloth or placemats. Place silverware and a napkin around each plate. Enjoy!

Leveling Up

Let the shrimp marinate for at least 15 minutes to absorb the flavors.

Add a touch of sweetness or depth to the sauce with one teaspoon of honey or 1 tablespoon of balsamic vinegar.

Add a small can (2 oz) of chopped black olives to the tomato/feta mix for extra color, texture, and interest.

Serve with crusty bread or a baguette to soak up the delicious juices.

Chapter 20

Beyond the Basics - Curry Dish

Guidelines for a Simple Curry

Ready to explore new flavors and impress your taste buds? This curry recipe is easy to prepare, even if some of the ingredients are new to you. You'll use an envelope of tamarind soup mix, which adds a unique tangy flavor that's sure to become a favorite. Shopping in the international aisle of your supermarket not only saves money but also opens up a world of culinary possibilities. Don't be afraid to step out of your comfort zone!

This curry is perfect for meal prepping and freezes well, making it a convenient option for busy weeks. It's also great for sharing with friends or roommates. Pair it with rice for a hearty meal, and feel free to stretch it further by adding extra vegetables, whether fresh or frozen. Enjoy the adventure of cooking and discover how delicious and satisfying homemade curry can be!

What You'll Need
-Large pot with a lid – a Dutch oven is ideal
-Non-stick pan with lid
-Large, graduated glass bowl with vented lid (Tool #3)
-Salad spinner (Tool #1)
-Can opener (Tool #4)
-Knife (Tool #6)
-Cutting board (Tool #7)
-Vegetable peeler (Tool #10)
-Pyrex measuring cup (Tool #8)

-Immersion blender (Tool #9)
-Large cooking spoon or ladle
-Paper towels

Ingredients
-Olive oil
-3 onions
-1 envelope Tamarind soup mix (1.41 oz)
-4 oz curry paste
-1 can of coconut milk (13-14 oz)
-4 cups of chicken broth (use a vegetable broth to make the dish vegetarian)
-1 block extra firm tofu (16 oz)
-2 cans chickpeas or garbanzo beans (16 oz each)
-2 cups shelled cashews (roasted is fine)
-8 carrots
-2 bunches cilantro (if you like it)
-1 potato
-Pepper

Step-by-Step Instructions:

Prepare the Tofu

Tofu is an economical and versatile protein option that easily absorbs flavors. To achieve a texture similar to chicken, pan-fry the tofu.

Pat dry a block of tofu with paper towels or a clean kitchen cloth. For extra moisture removal, wrap the tofu in a towel and press it between heavy books or use a tofu press if you have one.

Once dry, slice the tofu into 8 slices.

Heat 1 tablespoon of olive oil in a non-stick pan over medium heat.

Place the tofu slices in the pan and fry for 5-6 minutes on each side until browned.

Let the tofu cool, then dice it into cubes. Set aside in a large bowl.

Prepare the Onions

Dice 2 onions and set aside in a Dutch oven.

Slice the third onion into eighths and place it in a large bowl (but not with the tofu).

Prepare the Carrots

Peel and slice the carrots into rings or half-rings if they are large.

Add the sliced carrots to the bowl with the sliced onions.

Prepare the Chickpeas

Open 2 cans of chickpeas and drain the liquid using the spinner basket.

Add the chickpeas to the bowl with the tofu.

Prepare the Cilantro (Optional)

Wash the cilantro by adding 2 tablespoons of baking soda to the spinner bowl filled with cold water and swish the cilantro around to clean it.

Transfer to the spinner basket and spin dry.

Finely chop the cilantro and place half in the bowl with the tofu. Reserve the rest for garnish.

Prepare the Broth

Heat 2 cups of water in a microwave-safe Pyrex cup in the microwave.

Add enough bouillon to make 4 cups of broth (you will dilute it later by adding 2 more cups of water to the curry).

Prepare the Potato

Scrub a potato clean using a brush and baking soda. Keep the skin on for added nutrition.

Poke holes in the potato with a fork.

Place the potato on a plate and microwave on high for 5 minutes. Check for doneness by inserting a fork or knife; if not done, continue microwaving in 1-minute increments until tender.

Once done, set the potato aside to cool.

Start Cooking!

Add 2 tablespoons of olive oil to the onions, mix and heat at medium/low heat for about 15 minutes until softened.

Add the prepared broth, curry paste, coconut milk, tamarind soup mix, tofu, cashews, and chickpeas to the Dutch oven.

Add 10-15 turns of freshly crushed black pepper.

Let the mixture simmer for 1 hour.

While the curry is simmering, place the cooked potato in the now-empty tofu bowl. Add 2 cups of water and blend the potato into a paste using an immersion blender. If you need more liquid, ladle some from the curry pot.

Add the blended potato to the curry, which will act as a thickener.

Add the sliced onions and carrots to the curry and simmer for another 30-45 minutes, until the carrots are softened to your liking.

Serving Instructions

Spoon a generous portion of curry into a bowl or deep plate.

Serve over or alongside rice, ensuring each serving has a good mix of tofu, chickpeas, and vegetables.

Sprinkle the reserved cilantro on top.

Optionally, provide naan or roti in a separate basket or plate.

Storing Safely

Cool the Curry: Let the curry cool to room temperature before storing. This prevents condensation and helps maintain the food's quality.

Portion the Curry: Divide the curry into individual servings. This makes it easier to reheat only what you need.

Use Freezer Cubes for Efficient Storage

Place a portion of curry into each section of a silicone freezer cube tray.

Freeze the curry for 24 hours until solid.

Once frozen, pop the curry cubes out of the tray and transfer them to a labeled freezer bag. Include the contents and the date frozen on the label.

Simply take out the desired number of cubes and reheat when you're ready to enjoy your meal.

Chapter 21
Resources

Stock your Kitchen and More

The tools listed can be purchased at your local independent retailer.

For an electronic shopping list with links to national retailers, visit introtofood.com or email resources@introtofood.com.

Kitchen Kickstart Essential Tools
1. Salad spinner
2. Citrus juicer
3. Large, graduated glass bowl with vented lid
4. Manual can opener
5. Glass food storage with lids – assorted sizes
6. Knife set
7. Cutting boards
8. Pyrex measuring cups
9. Immersion blender with whisk attachment
10. Vegetable peeler

Essential Staples
1. Fresh lemons
2. Quality Bouillon/Broth
3. Grinding pepper
4. Table salt and Coarse salt for grinding
5. Quality pasta
6. Garlic fresh and in a jar

7. Baking soda
8. The Essential Oils: Extra Virgin and Pure Olive Oils
9. Dry minimally processed whole grains and legumes
10. Your favorite condiment (Ketchup, Mayo, Mustard, Hot Sauce, Pickles, etc.)

First Grocery Haul

Eggs: versatile for breakfast, lunch, or dinner.
Canned Protein: tuna, chicken, or other favorites for a quick protein boost.
Hearty Vegetables: carrots, cabbage, celery, kale, and other long-lasting veggies.
Canned Tomatoes: A base for sauces, soups, and stews.
Dry Lentils: a budget-friendly source of protein and fiber.
Onions: essential for adding flavor to almost any dish.
Rice: a filling, versatile grain that pairs well with many flavors.
Canned Beans: chickpeas, pinto beans, black beans for protein and fiber.
Potatoes: another versatile staple for side dishes or main courses.
Seasonal Fruits: apples, oranges, bananas for a healthy and delicious snack.

Beyond the Basics (as budget allows)

Drinks: coffee, tea, milk, cream, juice.
Dairy: milk, cheese (feta and grated parmesan), yogurt.
Pantry Staples: nuts, bread, cereal, jam, peanut butter.
Fresh Meat: ground beef/bison, chicken breasts.
Frozen: shrimp, fruits, vegetables.
Flavor Enhancers: Italian and Greek seasonings, Old Bay, Tajín, paprika, chili powder, onion powder, garlic powder, sweetener (sugar, honey, syrup).

Easy Measurement Table

Measurement	Equivalent
1 tablespoon (tbsp)	3 teaspoons (tsp)
1/4 cup	4 tablespoons (tbsp)
1/3 cup	5 tablespoons + 1 teaspoon
1/2 cup	8 tablespoons (tbsp)
2/3 cup	10 tablespoons + 2 teaspoons
3/4 cup	12 tablespoons (tbsp)
1 cup	16 tablespoons (tbsp)
1 pint (pt)	2 cups
1 quart (qt)	4 cups
1 gallon (gal)	4 quarts
1 ounce (oz)	2 tablespoons (tbsp)
1 pound (lb)	16 ounces (oz)
1 liter (L)	4.2 cups

Chapter 22

Notes

www.ingramcontent.com/pod-product-compliance
Lightning Source LLC
Chambersburg PA
CBHW050251010526
44107CB00003B/276